TOURISM: LEISURE AND RECREATION

TOURISM: LEISURE AND RECREATION

(In 3 Volumes)

(Tourism, Environment and the Society)
Volume 1

Editor
Sanchey Malviya

ISHA BOOKS
Delhi-110033

Tourism: Leisure and Recreation

(Tourism, Environment and the Society)

Rs. 2500 (Set)
Rs. 835 (Each Volume)

ISBN : 81-8205-213-0 (Set)
ISBN : 81-8205-313-7 (Vol. 1)

Published in 2005 in India by
Isha Books
D-43, Prithviraj Road,
Adarsh Nagar, Delhi - 110033
e-mail : ishabooks@hotmail.com

Laser Typesetting at : Global Printers, New Delhi
Printed at :
Rajdhani Printers, Ph. : 011-23215190

Contents

Preface

Tourism is the act of travel for the purpose of leisure, recreation, and the provision of services for this act. It is one of the world's largest industries and one of its fastest growing economic sectors. Many sovereignties, along with their respective countries and states, depend heavily upon travel expenditures by foreigners as a source of taxation and income for the enterprises that sell services to these travellers. Consequently the development of tourism is often a strategy employed either by a non-governmental organisation or a governmental agency to promote a particular region for the purpose of increasing commerce through exporting goods and services to non-locals.

Written for the use of students, researchers, professionals and policy planners in the field of tourism, the present publication elaborately narrates the major issues and concerns in this rapidly growing field. The first volume, *Tourism: Policies, Planning and Governance* is concerned with the planning and governance of tourism. The second volume, *Tourism, Environment and the Society* discusses the environmental and social impacts of tourism in detail. The third volume, *Tourism and Resource Management* describes various strategies to effectively manage tourism and its resources. This highly informative, authentic and up-to-date work will be interesting to all those concerned with tourism, leisure and recreation.

Editor

1
Tourism Trends

Tourism is the act of travel for the purpose of recreation, and the provision of services for this act. It is a service industry, comprising a number of tangible and intangible components. The tangible elements include transport systems — air, rail, road, water and now, space; hospitality services — accommodation, foods and beverages, tours, souvenirs; and related services such as banking, insurance and safety and security. The intangible elements include: rest and relaxation, culture, escape, adventure, new and different experiences. Many sovereignties, along with their respective countries and states, depend heavily upon travel expenditures by foreigners as a source of taxation and income for the enterprises that sellservices to these travellers. Consequently the development of tourism is often a strategy employed either by a non-governmental organization or a governmental agency to promote a particular region for the purpose of increasing commerce through exporting goods and services to non-locals.

Today, tourism is one of the world's largest industries and one of its fastest growing economic sectors. There were about 698 million international tourist arrivals worldwide in 2000, nearly 50 million more arrivals than in 1999 — the highest growth rate in nearly a decade. All regions in the world grew, and the fastest developing region continued to be East Asia and the Pacific with 14.6% growth, and 16% of the total market.

Europe saw an increase of 25 million international tourists, and had 57.7% of the market share - by far the largest among the world's regions. The Americas are the second-biggest region, with 18.5% of arrivals. International tourist receipts grew by 5%, totaling US$ 478 billion in 2000, with an additional US$ 97 billion from international transport carriers earned outside the country of origin. Receipts per arrival averaged US$ 700 in 1999. Air transport increased its share against road in international holidays; together these two account for 85% of all international trips. Rail and sea transport remain below 8% each.

Historical Development of Tourism

Wealthy people have always travelled to distant parts of the world to see great buildings or other works of art; to learn new languages; or to taste new cuisine. As long ago as the time of the Roman Republic places such as Baiae were popular coastal resorts for the rich. The terms tourist and tourism were first used as official terms in 1937 by the League of Nations. Tourism was defined as people travelling abroad for periods of over 24 hours.

The word tour gained acceptance in the 18th century, when the Grand Tour of Europe became part of the upbringing of the educated and wealthy British nobleman or cultured gentleman. Grand tours were taken in particular by young people to "complete" their education. They travelled all over Europe, but notably to places of cultural and aesthetic interest, such as Rome, Tuscany and the Alps.

The British aristocracy were particularly keen on the Grand Tour, using the occasion to gather art treasures from Europe to add to their collections. The volume of art treasures being moved to Britain in this way was unequalled anywhere else in Europe, and explains the richness of many private and public collections in Britain today. Yet tourism in those days, aimed essentially at the very top of the social ladder and at the well educated, was fundamentally a cultural activity. These first tourists, though undertaking their Grand Tour, were more travellers than tourists.

Most major British artists of the eighteenth century did the "Grand Tour", as did their great European contemporaries such as Claude Lorrain. Classical architecture, literature and art have always drawn visitors to Rome, Naples, Florence. The Romantic movement, extended this to Gothic countryside, the Alps, fast flowing rivers, mountain gorges, etc.

It was not until the 19th century that cultural tourism developed into leisure and health tourism. Some English travellers, after visiting the warm lands of the South of Europe, decided to stay there either for the cold season or for the rest of their lives. Others began to visit places with health-giving mineral waters, in order to relieve a whole variety of diseases from gout to liver disorders and bronchitis.

Leisure travel was a British invention due to sociological factors. Britain was the first European country to industrialize, and the industrial society was the first society to offer time for leisure to a growing number of people. Initially, this did not apply to the working masses, but rather to the owners of the machinery of production, the economic oligarchy, the factory owners, and the traders. These comprised the new middle class.

The British origin of this new industry is reflected in many place names. At Nice, one of the first and most well established holiday resorts on the French Riviera, the long esplanade along the seafront is known to this day as the Promenade des Anglais; in many other historic resorts in continental Europe, old well-established palace hotels have names like the Hotel Bristol, the Hotel Carlton or the Hotel Majestic - reflecting the dominance of English customers to whom these resorts previously catered to.

Even winter sports were largely invented by the British leisured classes initially at the Swiss village of Zermatt and St Moritz in 1864. Until the first tourists appeared, the Swiss thought of the long snowy winter as being a time when the best thing to do was to stay indoors and make cuckoo clocks or other small mechanical items.

The first packaged winter sports holidays followed in 1903, to Adelboden, also in Switzerland. Organized sport was well established in Britain before it reached other countries. The vocabulary of sport bears witness to this: rugby, football, and boxing all originated in Britain, and even Tennis, originally a French sport, was formalized and codified by the British, who hosted the first national championship in the nineteenth century, at Wimbledon. Winter sports were a natural answer for a leisured class looking for amusement during the coldest season.

Mass travel could not really begin to develop until two things occurred.

a) improvements in technology allowed the transport of large numbers of people in a short space of time to places of leisure interest, and

b) greater numbers of people began to enjoy the benefits of leisure time.

A major development was the invention of the railways, which brought many of Britain's seaside towns within easy distance of Britain's urban centres.

The father of modern mass tourism was Thomas Cook who, on 5 July 1841, organized the first package tour in history, by chartering a train to take a group of temperance campaigners from Leicester to a rally in Loughborough, some twenty miles away. Cook immediately saw the potential for business development in the sector, and became the world's first tour operator.

He was soon followed by others, with the result that the tourist industry developed rapidly in early Victorian Britain. Initially it was supported by the growing middle classes, who had time off from their work, and who could afford the luxury of travel and possibly even staying for periods of time in boarding houses.

However, the Bank Holiday Act 1871 introduced a statutory right for workers to take holidays, even if they were not paid at the time. The combination of short holiday periods, travel facilities and distances meant that the first holiday resorts to develop in Britain were towns on the seaside, situated as close as possible to the growing industrial conurbations.

For those in the industrial north, there were Blackpool in Lancashire, and Scarborough in Yorkshire. For those in the Midlands, there were Weston-super-Mare in Somerset and Skegness in Lincolnshire, for those in London there were Southend-on-Sea, Broadstairs, Brighton, Eastbourne, and a whole collection of other places.

In travelling to the coast, the population was following in the steps of Royalty. King George III is widely acknowledged as popularising the seaside holiday, due to his regular visits to Weymouth when in poor health.

For a century, domestic tourism was the norm, with foreign travel being reserved, as before, for the rich or the culturally curious. A minority of resorts, such as Bath,

Harrogate and Matlock, emerged inland. After World War II holiday villages such as Butlins and Pontins emerged, but their popularity waned with the rise of package tours and the increasing comforts to which visitors became accustomed at home. Towards the end of the 20th century the market was revived by the upmarket inland resorts of Dutch company Centre Parcs.

By 1901, the number of people crossing the English Channel from England to France or Belgium had passed 0.5 million per year. However it was with cheap air travel in combination with the package tour that international mass tourism developed after 1963. For the worker living in greater London, Brindisi today is almost as accessible as Brighton was 100 years ago.

There have been a few temporary setbacks in tourism, the latest being related to the September 11, 2001 attacks and terrorist threats to tourist destinations such as Bali and European cities. Some of the tourist destinations, including the Costa del Sol, the Baleares and Cancun have lost popularity due to shifting tastes and perceptions among tourists. In this context, the excessive building and environmental destruction often associated with traditional "sun and beach" tourism may contribute to a destination's saturation and subsequent decline. This appears to be the case with Spain's Costa Brava, a byword for this kind of tourism in the 1960s and 1970s. With only 11% of the Costa Brava now unblemished by low-quality development, the destination now faces a crisis in its tourist industry.

Belated attempts to move towards "quality tourism" are difficult given competition from cheaper, unspoilt holiday destinations on the one hand and the legacy of decades of over-exploitation on the other. In many respects, Tenerife provides a paradigm of the negative impact of mass tourism. Organizations like Greenpeace and ATAN are particularly critical of development on the island, arguing that Tenerife's current tourism industry is both economically and environmentally unsustainable. Receptive tourism is now growing at a very rapid rate in many developing countries, where it is often the most important economic activity in local GDP.

In recent years, second holidays or vacations have become more popular as people's disposable income increases. Typical combinations are a package to the typical mass tourist resort, with a winter skiing holiday or weekend break to a city or national park.

On 26 December 2004 a tsunami 2004 Indian Ocean earthquake hit Asian countries bordering the Indian Ocean, and also the Maldives. Tens of thousands of lives were lost, and many tourists died. This, together with the vast clean-up operation in place, has stopped or severely hampered tourism to the area.

The World Tourism Organization forecasts that international tourism will continue growing at the average annual rate of 4 percent. By 2020 Europe will remain the most popular destination, but its share will drop from 60 percent in 1995 to 46 percent. Long-haul will grow slightly faster than intraregional travel and by 2020 its share will increase from 18 percent in 1995 to 24 percent.

Space tourism is expected to "take off" in the first quarter of the 21st century, although compared with traditional destinations the number of tourists in orbit will remain low until technlogies such as space elevator make space travel cheap.Technological improvement is likely to make possible air-ship hotels, based either on solar-powered airplanes or large dirigibles. Underwater hotels, such as Hydropolis, slated to open in Dubai in 2006, will be built. On the surface of the ocean tourists will be welcomed by ever larger cruise ships and perhaps floating cities. Some futurists expect that movable hotel "pods" will be created that could be temporarily erected anywhere on the planet, where building a permanent resort would be unacceptable politically, economically or environ-mentally.

Tourism is one of s fast-growing sectors and is an increasing source of pressure on natural resources and the environment. Continuing growth may jeopardise the achievement of sustainable development and, unless properly managed, may affect the social conditions, cultures and local environment of tourist areas; it may also reduce the benefits of tourism to the local and wider economy. The main pressures come from transport, the use of water and land, energy use by buildings and facilities, and the generation of wastes. Erosion of soils and impacts on biodiversity are also tourism-related issues. In some popular destinations, these pressures have resulted in irreversible degradation of the local environment.

Tourism is the main driver behind the increase in the demand for passenger transport, with its associated environmental impacts. This demand is expected to continue to grow, including a significant contribution to doubling of air traffic over the next 20 years. Cars and planes, the most environmentally damaging modes, remain the most used forms of transport.

The high concentration and seasonal nature of tourism create some direct environmental impacts at destinations. The seaside and mountains remain the favourite destinations. Tourism is taking a growing share of household expenditure as relative prices continue to fall. There has been limited progress in the implementation of policies for more sustainable tourism, with minimal penetration of schemes such as eco-labelling within the tourism industry.

Tourism is increasingly seen as a sector that interacts strongly with other policies such as transport, environment, regional planning, energy, trade and business, and information technology. The sector is highly fragmented and has long been regarded as a local management issue. Until recently, there has been little policy attention at the national and international levels and little realisation of the need for more sustainable management.

Different countries have different institutional frameworks for tourism, from regional boards to state ministries, and some programmes that are designed to encourage sustainable tourism are being developed. However, most of the environmental measures that have so far been implemented have been initiated by major tour operators and local stakeholders and are based on voluntary approaches. There are examples of good practices in many countries (e.g. Austria, France, Germany, Spain, Switzerland and the United Kingdom) but most remain marginal (e.g. eco-label schemes or eco-taxes). There is a general lack of broad environmentally integrated strategies for the sector.

The tourism industry recognises the need to maintain its main assets, for example the attractiveness of destinations. While it is now generally recognised that tourism will be a successful industry only if it is managed in an ecological and sustainable manner, some efforts are still needed to move towards a broader and more integrated approach.

At the international level, the United Nations Commission on Sustainable Development (UNCSD) and the Convention on Biological Diversity (CBD) have targeted tourism as a priority policy area. At the regional level, the Mediterranean countries, the Alpine countries and the Baltic countries have initiated actions to promote sustainable tourism.

The European Union (EU) Council adopted a resolution in May 2002 on the need to improve the coordination of policies that affect tourism. An Agenda 21 programme includes an integrated evaluation of tourism activity throughout the EU, the development of an integration strategy for the sector and the elaboration of harmonised indicators of sustainable development for tourism.

Many factors affect the demand for tourism, including increases in time for leisure activities and their social importance, economic growth, and changes in demographic factors, behaviour and expectations. The choice of destination remains determined mainly by scenery and climate. Many countries offers the greatest diversity and density of attractions - coastal zones, islands, mountains, historical sites and countryside. Normally, tourists chose the sea, mountains, cities and the countryside as holiday destinations.

However, tourists are becoming more interested in higher quality tourism experiences, particularly in natural and cultural sites; nature, beauty and calm are the first criteria for choosing a destination, before price. During recent years, the length of vacations has increased, which gives more time for tourism and leisure. Europeans now take multiple holidays rather than extending the length of their main holiday. In the Netherlands for instance, the average number of vacations per person increased from 1.21 to 1.71 between 1966 and 1997, and the number of short breaks doubled in comparison to long vacations. UK residents who travelled within their own country spent 4.1 nights away from home on average in 1989 and 3.6 nights in 1997; most tourists now take short holidays. In France, the decrease in working hours, from 39 to 35 hours, has resulted in more days for holidays. There have been similar developments in several other countries.

Tourism, and particularly mass tourism to some destinations, has become more attractive and easily accessible as a result of more packaged holidays being on offer, strong marketing strategies, low prices and the developing use of the internet for reservations. All this has led to more journeys per person and per year. As people become more affluent and the relative costs of travel and holidays fall, tourism is taking a larger and larger share of household expenditure on leisure. The growth in tourism expenditure by households results mainly from the increase in transport, which accounts for the largest share of tourism expenditure.

Implications of Tourism

As one of the world's largest industries and one of its fastest growing economic sectors, tourism has a multitude of impacts, both positive and negative, on people's lives and on the environment. The quality of the environment, both natural and man-made, is essential to tourism. However, tourism's relationship with the environment is complex. It involves many activities that can have adverse environmental effects. Negative impacts from tourism will arise when the level of visitor use is superior to the environment's ability to cope with this use.

As tourism has become increasingly popular throughout the twentieth century, it has become increasingly influential in the global realm of social, economic, and environmental implications, however, not all of these impacts are positive in nature. Conversely, tourism can be detrimental to a community for a variety of reasons, as it tends to be a phenomenon that incorporates mass amounts of people in small places, which can cause pressure on both the culture and the environment in the area. Indeed, the existing forms of tourism activity, ranging from downhill skiing, development of coastal resorts, theme parks and golf courses, to increased visitor numbers to national parks and protected areas, have already brought about and continue to generate unmanaged environmental impacts. Such impacts include the loss of biodiversity and habitats, air and water pollution, noise and congestion, and increased competition for scarce resources.

However, it is not only the environment that suffers from tourism, as in many cases, the local people are often displaced from their homes, especially in developing countries, but in developed countries also, since they do not have the economic or political means to fight the powerful development corporations. Another issue of concern is that "tourism increases reliance upon a global economy, leaking many economic profits outside of the community back to the companies and countries that control most of the travel infrastructure,".

Local communities also tend to become dependent upon the tourism industries that are based there for subsistence, although the tourism industry is notoriously unreliable and unstable for a variety of reasons that are out of the community's control. For this reason, tourism does not offer stable or well-paid employment for the locals, making them increasingly vulnerable to the industry.

Tourism can have far-reaching and significant negative implications for the tourist destinations, from severe and diverse environmental degradation and destruction, to dominating financial interests of the industry and exploitation of the local peoples. Some believe that because of this, "tourism can destroy tourism; tourism as a user of resources can be a resource destroyer and, through destroying the resources which give rise to it, make resource-based tourism short-lived".

Uncontrolled coastal tourism development poses potential threats to many natural areas around the world as it can put enormous pressure on a very narrow area. Many of these impacts are linked with the construction of general infrastructure such as roads and airports, and of tourism facilities, including resorts, hotels, restaurants, shops, golf courses and marinas. Such developments often lead to impacts such as soil erosion, increased pollution, waste discharges into the sea, natural habitat loss and associated loss in biodiversity and increased pressure on endangered species. This is particularly true for some of the world's most ecologically fragile areas such as wetlands, mangroves, coral reefs and sea grass beds. Furthermore, it often puts a strain on water resources, and it can force local populations to compete for the use of critical resources such as fish. By involving many activities that can have adverse environmental effects tourism has the potential to gradually destroy the environmental resources on which it depends. Usually these effects are dynamic and often interactive.

On the other hand, tourism has the potential to create beneficial effects on the environment by contributing to environmental protection and conservation. It is a way to raise awareness of environmental values and it can serve as a tool to finance protection of natural areas and increase their economic importance.

Tourism and the Changing World

Economy

The world economy is growing and there is increased affluence. Rising incomes will allow people to spend more money on leisure activities. Tourism is predicted to grow substantially in the coming years, with the annual world spend on all leisure and business travel expected to double to 3 trillion over the next 10 years. Although there is greater growth, there is also increasing disparity of wealth and a growing polarisation in the distribution of income i.e. the rich will become richer and the poor will become poorer in the years to come. Substantial poverty still exists in the world with over a quarter of the world"s population still living on less than $1/day.

The European Monetary Union and the removal of the need for currency exchange will reduce the cost of travelling further and should establish a free flow of tourism in Europe. A UK decision to opt out could be detrimental to Scottish tourism in the short term. European holiday destinations are losing market share as new destinations and competitors emerge, however increased affluence world wide will mean tourism to Europe will continue to grow.

Technology

Ten per cent of the world"s population will have access to the Internet within five years. Over 11,000 new users a day surf the internet in the UK, whilst in France internet use is growing at a rate of 7% per month. In Europe the travel-on-line market is forecasted to be the fastest growing sector over the next few years.

E-commerce (paying over the internet) will represent 1 in 8 of travel industry transactions in 2003. The internet is already changing the way consumers access and book the holiday product. The increasing use of the internet for e-commerce will provide new opportunities to sell accommodation and other tourism related products.

Improved access by customers to information on tourism products will make it easier for them to compare quality and prices on an international basis. The internet is increasingly being used to find the best deals with the travel agent being cut out.

The increase in digital and interactive television coupled with mobile phone technology advances will allow more and more people to access the internet. New technology will shift the power from tourism businesses to consumers who will increasingly use it to source deals and will expect tailor-made, customised tourist information. New technology has the potential to provide new opportunities and facilitate ease of access to and from customers. The increased opportunity will be tempered by the risk of increased ''noise'' from competitors and other sources.

Environment

Climatic changes will evolve quite slowly and although the exact impact of climatic change is open to debate, the initial impacts are expected to include:

— Temperatures are predicted to increase over Scotland by up to 1C in 2020. There will be more warming in winter than in summer, with autumn and winter becoming wetter.

— Rainfall will increase by around 5% by 2020. More frequent intense daily rainfall events are also expected, and an increase in severe winter gales.

— There will be a rise in sea levels as a result of the melting of polar ice caps. Scottish sea levels are predicted to rise by 2cm by the 2050s.

— There will be increased flooding due to a combination of sea level rise, increased rainfall and increased thaw rates of mountain snow and ice. The most vulnerable areas are the Forth, Clyde and Tay lowlands, Deeside and the Dornoch Firth.

A change in climate and habitats will place direct pressure on mountain sports, such as skiing and shooting. Changes in temperature, precipitation and wind speed could have a dramatic effect upon land cover with a subsequent knock-on effect on habitats and wildlife. The major short-term impact of the environment will be on consumer''s tastes and demands with a higher awareness of green issues and an increasing importance attached to a pollution-free, green environment and environmentally sensitive ways of running businesses. There is increasing evidence that consumers are willing to pay more for products and services with environmental benefits.

Transport and Political

Growing road congestion will increase the appeal of Scotland as a place for car touring away from the crowds. Road pricing and taxes on fuel and car use will make it more expensive to do so. Scottish regional airports will have better access than ever to Europe. The development of the East Coast and West main railway lines, improvements in air access and the proposed Scotland to Europe direct ferry will open up new markets and allow us to develop new products and packages. Political or legislative events which are expected to have an impact on the tourism industry include the enlargement of the EU, duty free legislation, working time directive, VAT harmonisation measures and, of course, the potential for conflict in Europe.

Ageing Population

People are living longer than ever before especially in developed western economies. In the UK Over 65s will rise from 16% (9m) to 20% (12m) of the population in the next 20 years.In Germany, 16% of the population is aged 65 or over and this is expected to increase to 20% in the next 10 years. In France people over 60 account for 16% of the population and this is expected to rise to 20% in

2020. It is predicted that a fifth of the population of Europe being aged 65 or over in 2020.

This market will be more active than in previous generations and may well choose to continue working past traditional retirement age. They will not abandon leisure and health activities when they retire and they will expect the range of offers and level of service that a lifetime of consumerism has accustomed them to.

The growing population of older people will initially create larger target markets for Scotland who have the time and disposable income to travel.

These visitors will be better travelled than previous generations and more willing to travel but they will also be more aware of our competition and may therefore be harder to attract.

They will have the time to take holidays throughout the year, will be more "experience" than destination focused and will demand quality of product and service as standard. Their "experience" focus may mean greater scope for specialist or niche markets like soft, accessible activities.

Global Trends

Whether one is marketing a complete tourism destination, a specific tourism activity within a destination (such as wildlife viewing or hiking) or simply one or two visitor products within a destination, it is important that one does not market from within a limited scope or target market awareness. It is vitally important that there is an understanding and cognizance of the global, national and regional tourism trends as well as any shifts in travel patterns, purchasing processes or demographics and psychographics as they pertain to a destination's target markets.

The travelling consumer of the here and now is very different from any other time in history. The most successful in the travel industry are those that respond to the challenge through the use of technology, innovative marketing programs, better training of staff and by developing a closeness and understanding of its customers/guests. The differences in travel patterns in the next century will be more related to what consumers are seeking in a travel experience than in how they travel.

In the effort to provide up-to-date and relevant tourism statistics and trends from a global perspective, accessing timely statistics has always been a challenge. Without question, one organization that collects and collates pertinent tourism data is the World Tourism Organization (WTO) and affiliated organizations such as The Travel Research Association (TTRA).

During the past few years a series of dramatic events around the world is changing the global, political and cultural environment in a way that is certain to effect the future growth and prosperity of the international tourism industry. These events include, but are not limited to: a new accord between Russia and China; the signing of the NAFTA agreement; the end of apartheid in Africa; the emergence of North Korea as an economic powerhouse; the government liberalization program in India; a cease fire in Northern Ireland; the signing of peace accords between Israel, Jordan and Palestine; an intense civil war in the once Yugoslavia; continuing civil wars in Africa, Southeast Asia and Cambodia, etc.

Most economists agree that there is a close correlation between the growth of a nation's economy and the amount of travel generated by its citizens. Today, the economic news from most regions of the world is strongly positive. With most of the world's population living in countries that are showing substantial economic growth, the last half of the 90s' was a bright period in the history of world tourism.

In short, while there are many international issues worthy of serious concern, the overall growth and stabilization of emerging economies bode well for global tourism growth.

Without getting into an intense level of detail, to follow is a brief synopsis of global tourism trends:

— gross output of the world's domestic and international tourism industry in 1994 was estimated to have reached $3.4 trillion. This includes $2 trillion spent by consumers, $352 billion by governments, $401 billion by business, and capital investment of $693 billion. These estimates indicate that tourism is without doubt the world's largest industry;

— world-wide international arrivals in 1993 increased by 3.4% to 500 million (WTO);

— in the United States in 1993 inbound foreign visitor arrivals declined 3.7% to 45.8 million. This was the first decline in nine years. Canadian arrivals were down by 6.9% while arrivals from overseas countries were up by 4.9%;

— in 1993, outbound Americans travelling to foreign countries increased 1.1% to 44.4 million. Travellers visiting Canada were up by 1.5% and travellers to Mexico declined by 5.1%. US travellers visiting other overseas countries were up 7.1%; and

— in 1993 the Americas reported arrivals up 5.3% to 106.5 million, with receipts up 4.7% to $87.5 billion. There was a strong increase in arrivals from Europe.

In addition to the above statistics, how people travel and what people are looking for in travel destinations has been changing on a fairly consistent basis for the past decade. The "greening" of people's attitudes world-wide, leads to the following tourism trends.

Over the next ten years, tourism products and attractions will have to cater to visitors who are more demanding and discriminating, as well as more active and more purposeful in their choice of destination. There will be a shift in emphasis from passive fun to active learning, and the quality and genuineness of visitor experiences will be crucial to future success in a competitive market.

Key shifts in global tourism market trends are summarized below:

— in the long term, the average standard of living in western developed countries will increase, as will the amount of discretionary money available for travel;

— rising affluence will bring with it increases in the amount of free time available. Longer weekends and increased paid holidays have helped to stimulate expansion in attraction visitation;

— there is a shift in emphasis from passive fun to active learning;

— activity or special interest holidays are likely to gain at the expense of conventional sightseeing, visiting and other passive experiences;

— there is growing concern about the impact of modern industry, including tourism, on the physical and social environment;

— there is growing awareness of risks to personal health and safety;

— leisure time will be used more actively, for mental development as well as physical exercise;

— people aged 45 to 64 years of age will be growing significantly in number to the year 2010. In the United

States alone, this age group is forecasted to grow by 31% by the year 2000;

— the potential visitor of the future will be: older, more affluent; more demanding; more thoughtful and discriminating; and more active physically and mentally;

— decision making windows will be smaller. Hence, one-stop-shopping for all-inclusive packages will continue to be appealing; and

— consumers will increasingly seek low impact tourism facilities, consistent with environmental values and the desire not to contribute to negative impacts.

Ecotourism one of the more popular sector of tourism, is an industry that has been experiencing rapid growth in the last few decades. The World Tourism Organization (WTO) "claims that tourism is currently the world's largest industry, with annual revenues of almost $3 trillion, its economic impact is second only to the weapons industry,".

As tourism has grown globally, its impacts have also grown, having as increasing impact on the economy and also on the environment. Tourism has many global implications, as travel is frequently international, including both countries of the North and the South. Tourism is especially important in developing nations as it "is seen as a way to propel regional economic growth in countries, a panacea for development...[as] tourism promises jobs, economic growth in countries and infrastructure development,".

Many developing nations, for these reasons, strive to maintain or increase their tourist attractions as tourism has such a huge impact in many areas in the economy. The importance of tourism is not unique to developing nations, though, in generating significant sources of profits.

Factors that will Shape Tourism in the Future

The travel and tourism buzzword of the 21st century will be the search for balance. The identification, maintenance and management of this threshold of balance will be the single most important requirement for the tourism industry of the 21st century. Those companies, institutions and destinations that perform the balancing act well will attain that elusive goal of sustainable development. Those that don't, or won't, will be trapped forever in vicious boom and bust cycles.

This balancing act will manifest itself strongly as the following critical issues and trends play out throughout the travel and tourism industry in the 21st century.

1. *Economic impact and leakage from tourism:* Set to become probably the most significant hot-potato issue in the early 21st century. Governments will be seeking to maximise that economic impact by first keeping more earnings at home and after that, within the region. That will run up against the increased advances of global multinational groups which will be sending more and more money out in the form of franchise, distribution, management fees and various other forms of earnings.

2. *Extension of U.S. influence throughout the travel and tourism industry:* The most visible signs of U.S. presence are movies, fast-food chains, hotels, air-lines, theme-parks, credit card companies, media and Internet distribution technology Over the next two years, these prominent signs of U.S. presence will grow throughout Pacific Asia through equity deals, management and franchise contracts. As tourism is a high-profile industry, the response from local com-munities could well be unpredictable, especially in places where such images are not popular.

3. *Impact of globalisation*: Related to the above but impacting on Other issues like environmental and

consumer protection regulations, changes in currency (such as the recent implementation of the euro) and aviation policies.

4. *Greater liberalisation of visas, border control formalities and investment opportunities.* Several major regional caucuses like the Asia-Pacific Economic Cooperation and ASEAN have this triumvirate of issues on their agendas in view of the recognition that they are major impediments to the flow of people and goods. Step by step, these barriers will fall as countries adjust to the new realities. However, it is critically important to ensure that the countries are encouraged, not pushed, to make the changes.

5. *Taxation*: Countries, states and even cities that give tax breaks to the tourism industry are advertising it as a promotional tool. In many countries, there is a tendency to do the opposite, i.e. to tax travel and tourism because visitors don't vote. That is a fallacy; visitors vote with their feet. They go else-where. Monitoring mechanisms like the WTTC's Tax Barometer are keeping a watch on these tax increases in the form of a performance score-card. In the latest barometer, released at WTM, Asian destinations hit by currency evaluations did not fare well, mainly because they had to adjust various airport taxes in line with the extent of the devaluation.

6. *Social issues*: The hardest work for the industry lies in convincing its constituents that it is not an industry by the rich for the rich. In many parts of the world, luxury hotels are still an incongruous embarrassment in the midst of surrounding poverty Either ostentation will have to be replaced by modesty or the industry will have to work harder at explaining why it is paying housekeepers as much as it charges guests for 20 cups of coffee. Non-governmental organisations still blame

travel and tourism for abetting the problem of child prostitution, even though the industry is working very hard to combat it.

7. *Employment*: As the industry gains greater respectability and recognition, it will attract more than its fair share of qualified young people seeking to see the world and enjoy the sights and sounds they are exposed to over the Internet. Mobility will increase as Internet web sites allow people to find work in different parts of the world. There will be great demand for people with language skills and ability to work in different cultures.

8. *Safety concerns, crime and political problems, including terrorism, will dominate agendas.* In 1998, many tourist destinations suffered from such problems, leading to a marked increase in visitor arrivals in places free of them. Some countries capitalised on the woes of their competitors to stress their political and economic safety in an attempt to regain market share. The struggle to come up with effective crisis management scenarios for the tourism industry continues.

9. *Influence of organised crime*: There is growing evidence that the cash-rich status of the industry is a convenient channel for global money-laundering rackets, especially through casinos, real estate deals and purchases of luxury items. This is attracting the interest of law enforcement officers and will he the subject of many a media scandal as prominent investors are identified as potential suspects.

10. *Technology*: It is now all but accepted that travel agents are going to become just a regular part of the distribution equation and will have to earn their keep based on their productivity for a supplier New multi-channel strategies being announced by airlines, and soon to be followed by hotels, will involve distributing

their products through the Internet, direct sales, frequent flyer databases, corporate suppliers and agents. As one European airline said in announcing the new strategy, "In a world where 100 percent of our frequent travellers have a cellular telephone, 85 percent have a PC and over 50 percent are surfing the Internet a number of times each week, we must adapt our distribution to these new conditions."

11. *Environmental issues*: The travel industry has clearly got the message that a strong environmental ethic is at the heart of its survival. Hotel chains, airlines and tour operators are responding energetically to calls for the industry to protect the long-term viability of its lifeline. Travel and tourism's main problem will be the environmental impact of other polluting industries in the neighbourhood.

12. *Airlines and aviation*: The global power of the airline alliances will begin to manifest itself, parlaying into code-sharing, joint purchasing, database marketing and more alliances with the smaller airlines of Asia. While traffic will take time to recover, capacity has also been reduced due to the huge number of deferred aircraft orders. Airlines are in a heavier cost-cutting mood than ever before. The best that the industry can hope for is that those airlines which cut routes in 1997/98 will reinstate them this year No new destinations are expected to be added. Privatisation of both airports and airlines will continue.

13. *Across-the-board alliances between the public and private sectors, as well as amongst them.* As access to databases becomes critical, and direct marketing becomes the rage, these alliances will drive the industry as all participants in it seek to attain the highest common denominator One interesting trend is the growing link between tourism and its associate/supportive

industries such as agriculture, textiles, gems and jewelry, retailing and even arts/culture.

14. *Hotels*: Hotels can brace for major take-overs and expansion efforts by the brand-name U.S.- owned chains, especially franchise operators whose offers will be difficult to resist or refuse. As branding gains strength, the unbranded may find themselves increasingly isolated. Branded hotels will receive the backing of marketing and networking power In the U.S., some branded hotels are also receiving low-interest or no-interest loans to help them with renovations. But terms and conditions are strict.

15. *Cruise and marine tourism*: Will take off in a big way throughout the rivers, seas and oceans. But major upgrading of standards and improved facilitation will be necessary if countris will compete with each other. In the U.K., British Waterways conducted research on how people escape from stress and found that over a quarter of a million people will take a canal boat holiday in the U.K. in 1998 and that canal boating is twice as popular as a day at an amusement park and just as attractive as a weekend at the seaside.

16. *Trade shows*: The clutter of international trade shows will continue but break up into smaller niche-market shows focusing on both countries and product category This will open up opportunities for buyers to specialise in various segments but also run the risk of putting their eggs in one bas-ket.

17. *Greater focus on regional promotions:* To stretch their promotional dollars, groupings such as the South Pacific and Indian Ocean islands, Mekong region countries, African states and others will be stepping up pooling of resources to undertake joint marketing and research efforts. At the WTM, groupings like Caribbean Tourism had a prominent profile, especially as they

were seeking to regain mar-ket share of the devastating hurricanes of the previous September and November. Other banners are also emerging, such as the Silk Road.

18. *Emergence of the Middle East:* Likely to start running out of oil over the next 20 to 30 years, and with no other resources to sell, many Middle Fast countries are gradually turning to tourism, capitalism on their historic cultures and Islamic traditions. One major U.K. tour operator announced the start of the first tours to Saudi Arabia. Dubai is as usual at the forefront and will play a prominent role in guiding the tourism destinies of other Gulf countries.

19. *Growth in religious tourism*: The publicity and promotion of the Bethlehem 2000 project commemorate the birth of Christ is expected to be the major catalyst for a revival in religious tourism globally Areas such as the Buddhist circuit in India and major religious icons like Angkor Wat are only some of the thousands of significant religious spots throughout the Pacific Asia region that could benefit. Holiday patterns, too, are heading in that direction. Holidays were once purely recreational but in the last 10 years have moved into physical and mental rejuvenation. Spiritual rejuvenation is quite likely to be next.

20. *Holiday trends*: A recent study undertaken by the World Tourism Organization on the impact of global economic changes on employment and holiday-taking patterns concluded that there would be a trend towards more and shorter holidays against fewer and longer holidays, mainly due to time constraints and job insecurities. Though labour laws and working conditions in many countries are moving towards giving more free time, corporate downsizing is leading many executives to work overtime anyway, mostly at home.

21. *Emergence of secondary cities, both as source and destinations*. So far, most of the world's tourists have originated in the major cities and headed for the major cities, usually as an initial stop-ping off point en route to somewhere else. However, worldwide, there are hundreds of state and provincial capitals with sizeable populations, all seeking to get a piece of the action. As these cities emerge from the backwaters, increasing airline and transportation links will help them become inbound/outbound mar-kets in their own right.

2
Environmental Impacts

Tourism continues to grow rapidly, and is expected to increase by 4 per cent each year over the next five years. It is expanding in all regions, including in remote and sensitive areas. Tourism relationship with the environment is complex. Given its scale and global extent, it is inevitable that tourism has important environmental impacts. These impacts are related to resource consumption, as well as to pollution and waste generated by tourism activities, including impacts from transport. At the same time, beaches and mountains, rivers, forests and biodiversity make the environment a basic resource upon which the tourism industry depends to thrive and grow, and threats to the environment threaten the viability of the tourism industry. Lastly, tourism can contribute to environmental protection.

Tourism has a multitude of impacts, both positive and negative, on people's lives and on the environment. The quality of the environment, both natural and man-made, is essential to tourism. However, tourism's relationship with the environment is complex. It involves many activities that can have adverse environmental effects. Many of these impacts are linked with the construction of general infrastructure such as roads and airports, and of tourism facilities, including resorts, hotels, restaurants, shops, golf courses and marinas. The negative impacts of tourism development can gradually destroy the environmental resources on which it depends. On the other hand, tourism has the potential to create beneficial effects on the environment by contributing to environmental protection and conservation. It is a way to raise awareness of environmental values and it can serve as a tool to finance protection of natural areas and increase their economic importance.

Main Impact Areas

Negative impacts from tourism occur when the level of visitor use is greater than the environment's ability to cope with this use within the acceptable limits of change. Uncontrolled conventional tourism poses potential threats to many natural areas around the world. It can put enormous pressure on an area and lead to impacts such as soil erosion, increased pollution, discharges into the sea, natural habitat loss, increased pressure on endangered species and heightened vulnerability to forest fires. It often puts a strain on water resources, and it can force local populations to compete for the use of critical resources.

Deletion of Natural Resources

Tourism development can put pressure on natural resources when it increases consumption in areas where resources are already scarce.

Water resources

Water, and especially fresh water, is one of the most critical natural resources. The tourism industry generally overuses water resources for hotels, swimming pools, golf courses and personal use of water by tourists. This can result in water shortages and degradation of water supplies, as well as generating a greater volume of waste water.

In dryer regions like the Mediterranean, the issue of water scarcity is of particular concern. Because of the hot climate and the tendency of tourists to consume more water when on holiday than they do at home, the amount used can run up to 440 liters a day. This is almost double what the inhabitants of an average Spanish city use.

Golf course maintenance can also deplete fresh water resources. In recent years golf tourism has increased in popularity and the number of golf courses has grown rapidly. Golf courses require an enormous amount of water every day and, as with other causes of excessive extraction of water, this can result in water scarcity. If the water comes from wells, overpumping can cause saline intrusion into groundwater. Golf resorts are more and more often situated in or near protected areas or areas where resources are limited, exacerbating their impacts.

An average golf course in a tropical country such as Thailand needs 1500kg of chemical fertilizers, pesticides and herbicides per year and uses as much water as 60,000 rural villagers.

Local resources

Tourism can create great pressure on local resources like energy, food, and other raw materials that may already be in short supply. Greater extraction and transport of these resources exacerbates the physical impacts associated with their exploitation. Because of the seasonal character of the industry, many destinations have ten times more inhabitants in the high season as in the low season. A high demand is placed upon these resources to meet the high expectations tourists often have (proper heating, hot water, etc.).

Land degradation

Important land resources include minerals, fossil fuels, fertile soil, forests, wetland and wildlife. Increased construction of tourism and recreational facilities has increased the pressure on these resources and on scenic landscapes. Direct impact on natural resources, both renewable and nonrenewable, in the provision of tourist facilities can be caused by the use of land for accommodation and other infrastructure provision, and the use of building materials. Forests often suffer negative impacts of tourism in the form of deforestation caused by fuel wood collection and land clearing. For example, one trekking tourist in Nepal - and area already suffering the effects of deforestation - can use four to five kilograms of wood a day.

Harm to wildlife and habitats

The main harm to wildlife and habitats is:

— *Biological resources*: disruption of wildlife habitats, clearance of vegetation for tourism developments, increased pressure on endangered species due to trade and hunting; extra demand for fuelwood, forest fires

— *Ecologically fragile areas*: such as rain forests, wetlands, mangroves, coral reefs, sea grass beds. If not properly planned and managed nature tourism threatens the world's most ecologically fragile areas including parks and natural world heritage sites

Pollution

Tourism can cause the same forms of pollution as any other industry: air emissions, noise, solid waste and littering, releases of sewage, oil and chemicals, even architectural/visual pollution.

Air and noise pollution

Transport by air, road, and rail is continuously increasing in response to the rising number of tourists and their greater mobility. To give an indication, the ICAO reported that the number of international air passengers worldwide rose from 88 million in 1972 to 344 million in 1994. One consequence of this increase in air transport is that tourism now accounts for more than 60% of air travel and is therefore responsible for an important share of air emissions. One study estimated that a single transatlantic return flight emits almost half the CO_2 emissions produced by all other sources (lighting, heating, car use, etc.) consumed by an average person yearly.

Transport emissions and emissions from energy production and use are linked to acid rain, global warming and photochemical pollution. Air pollution from tourist transportation has impacts on the global level, especially from carbon dioxide (CO_2) emissions related to transportation energy use. And it can contribute to severe local air pollution. Some of these impacts are quite specific to tourist activities. For example, especially in very hot or cold countries, tour buses often leave their motors running for hours while the tourists go out for an excursion because they want to return to a comfortably air-conditioned bus.

Noise pollution from airplanes, cars, and buses, as well as recreational vehicles such as snowmobiles and jet skis, is an ever-growing problem of modern life. In addition to causing annoyance, stress, and even hearing loss for it humans, it causes distress to wildlife, especially in sensitive areas. For instance, noise generated by snowmobiles can cause animals to alter their natural activity patterns.

Solid waste and littering

In areas with high concentrations of tourist activities and appealing natural attractions, waste disposal is a serious problem and improper disposal can be a major despoiler of the natural environment - rivers, scenic areas, and roadsides. For example, cruise ships in the Caribbean are estimated to produce more than 70,000 tons of waste each year. Today some cruise lines are actively working to reduce waste-related impacts. Solid waste and littering can degrade the physical appearance of the water and shoreline and cause the death of marine animals.

In mountain areas, trekking tourists generate a great deal of waste. Tourists on expedition leave behind their garbage, oxygen cylinders and even camping equipment. Such practices degrade the environment with all the detritus typical of the developed world, in remote areas that have few garbage collection or disposal facilities. Some trails in the Peruvian Andes and in Nepal frequently visited by tourists have been nicknamed "Coca-Cola trail" and "Toilet paper trail".

Sewage

Construction of hotels, recreation and other facilities often leads to increased sewage pollution. Wastewater has polluted seas and lakes surrounding tourist attractions, damaging the flora and fauna. Sewage runoff causes serious damage to coral reefs because it stimulates the growth of algae, which cover the filter-feeding corals, hindering their ability to survive. Changes in salinity and siltation can have wide-ranging impacts on coastal environments. And sewage pollution can threaten the health of humans and animals.

Aesthetic Pollution

Often tourism fails to integrate its structures with the natural features and indigenous architectural of the destination. Large, dominating resorts of disparate design can look out of place in any natural environment and may clash with the indigenous structural design.

A lack of land-use planning and building regulations in many destinations has facilitated sprawling developments along coastlines, valleys and scenic routes. The sprawl includes tourism facilities themselves and supporting infrastructure such as roads, employee housing, parking, service areas, and waste disposal.

Impacts on Islands and Coastal Areas

In islands and coastal areas, the main types of pollution in coastal waters resulting from tourism include sediment run off, sewage, solid waste, high nutrient loads, synthetic organic chemicals, oil, and pathogens. These result in eutrophication, and deteriorating of water quality, which have adverse effects on coastal ecosystems and their living resources, and so impair their value for tourism as well as other uses. This is in particular the case of coral reefs that are at high risk world-wide Tourism development can be intensive on coastal fringes and has caused major damage to coastal ecosystems. For example, three-quarters of the sand dunes on the Mediterranean coastline from Spain to Sicily have disappeared mainly as a result of urbanisation linked to tourism development.

Development of new berths for cruise ships can destroy valuable coastal habitats and their massive anchors and chains have for instance gouged large chasms three to nine meters deep in parts of the Caribbean.

Because of island characteristics and limitations of resources, adverse environmental effects from tourism may have more immediate repercussions than elsewhere, as highlighted by the Conference on "Sustainable Tourism in Small Island Developing States and Other Islands, organised in October 1998 by UNEP and WTO in Lanzarote, Canary Islands, Spain.

Impacts on mountain regions

Mountain regions and communities often have fragile environments and socio-economic relations, the latter frequently important factors in environmental management. Problems associated with tourism in mountain regions include: sewage pollution of rivers, sedimentation and emissions from construction activities, erosion and landslides linked to trails and skiing/ snowmobiling, water extraction from streams to supply resorts, damage to habitats during construction and use, interruption by roads and construction of animal migration between life zones, litter accumulation on trails. In North America, awareness is growing within the skiing industry of its effects on mountain environments and of the benefits from applying sound environmental management practices.

Environmental management of ski areas on federal government lands in Canada and the United States have also helped to set standards. In many mountain areas, concern has grown about the negative impacts of tourism on the natural environment, village economies and cultural traditions. The Annapurna Conservation Area Project, in Nepal, has been set up to address such concerns by practising multiple land use methods of resource management combined with sustainable community development. All activities are carried out with the full participation of local people and communities making them guardians of their resources, and are designed to ensure that local people benefit from trekking tourism and conservation.

Physical Impacts

Attractive landscape sites, such as sandy beaches, lakes, riversides, and mountain tops and slopes, are often transitional zones, characterized by species-rich ecosystems. Typical physical impacts include the degradation of such ecosystems.

An ecosystem is a geographic area including all the living organisms, their physical surroundings, and the natural cycles that sustain them. The ecosystems most threatened with degradation are ecologically fragile areas such as alpine regions, rain forests, wetlands, mangroves, coral reefs and sea grass beds. The threats to and pressures on these ecosystems are often severe because such places are very attractive to both tourists and developers.

In industrial countries, mass tourism and recreation are now fast overtaking the extractive industries as the largest threat to mountain communities and environments. Since 1945, visits to the 10 most popular mountainous national parks in the United States have increased twelve-fold. In the European Alps, tourism now exceeds 100 million visitor-days. Every year in the Indian Himalaya, more than 250,000 Hindu pilgrims, 25,000 trekkers, and 75 mountaineering expeditions climb to the sacred source of the Ganges River, the Gangotri Glacier. They deplete local forests for firewood, trample riparian vegetation, and strew litter. Even worse, this tourism frequently induces poorly planned, land-intensive development.

Physical impacts are caused not only by tourism-related land clearing and construction, but by continuing tourist activities and long-term changes in local economies and ecologies.

Physical impacts of tourism development

— *Construction activities and infrastructure development*: The development of tourism facilities such as accommodation, water supplies, restaurants and recreation facilities can involve sand mining, beach and sand dune erosion, soil erosion and extensive paving. In addition, road and airport construction can lead to land degradation and loss of wildlife habitats and deterioration of scenery.

In Yosemite National Park (US), for instance, the number of roads and facilities have been increased to keep pace with the growing visitor numbers and to supply amenities, infrastructure and parking lots for all these tourists. These actions have caused habitat loss in the park and are accompanied by various forms of pollution including air pollution from automobile emissions; the Sierra Club has reported "smog so thick that Yosemite Valley could not be seen from airplanes". This occasional smog is harmful to all species and vegetation inside the Park.

— *Deforestation and intensified or unsustainable use of land:* Construction of ski resort accommodation and facilities frequently requires clearing forested land. Coastal wetlands are often drained and filled due to lack of more suitable sites for construction of tourism facilities and infrastructure. These activities can cause severe disturbance and erosion of the local ecosystem, even destruction in the long term.

— *Marina development:* Development of marinas and breakwaters can cause changes in currents and coastlines. Furthermore, extraction of building materials such as sand affects coral reefs, mangroves, and hinterland forests, leading to erosion and destruction of habitats. In the Philippines and the Maldives, dynamiting and mining of coral for resort building materials has damaged fragile coral reefs and depleted the fisheries that sustain local people and attract tourists.

Overbuilding and extensive paving of shorelines can result in destruction of habitats and disruption of land-sea connections (such as sea-turtle nesting spots).

— Coral reefs are especially fragile marine ecosystems and are suffering worldwide from reef-based tourism developments. Evidence suggests a variety of impacts to coral result from shoreline development, increased sediments in the water, trampling by tourists and divers, ship groundings, pollution from sewage, overfishing, and fishing with poisons and explosives that destroy coral habitat.

Physical impacts from tourist activities

— *Trampling*: Tourists using the same trail over and over again trample the vegetation and soil, eventually causing damage that can lead to loss of biodiversity and other impacts. Such damage can be even more extensive when visitors frequently stray off established trails.

Trampling impacts on vegetation	Trampling impacts on soil
Breakage and bruising of stems	Loss of organic matter
Reduced plant vigor	Reduction in soil macro porosity
Reduced regeneration	Decrease in air and water permeability
Loss of ground cover	Increase in run off
Change in species composition	Accelerated erosion

— *Anchoring and other marine activities:* In marine areas (around coastal waters, reefs, beach and shoreline, offshore waters, uplands and lagoons) many tourist activities occur in or around fragile ecosystems. Anchoring, snorkeling, sport fishing and scuba diving, yachting, and cruising are some of the activities that can cause direct degradation of marine ecosystems such as coral reefs, and subsequent impacts on coastal protection and fisheries.

— *Alteration of ecosystems by tourist activities:* Habitat can be degraded by tourism leisure activities. For example, wildlife viewing can bring about stress for the animals and alter their natural behavior when tourists come too close. Safaris and wildlife watching activities have a degrading effect on habitat as they often are accompanied by the noise and commotion created by tourists as they chase wild animals in their trucks and aircraft. This puts high pressure on animal habits and behaviors and tends to bring about behavioral changes. In some cases, as in Kenya, it has led to animals becoming so disturbed that at times they neglect their young or fail to mate.

Loss of Biodiversity

Biological diversity is the term given to the variety of life on Earth and the natural patterns it forms.

The effects of loss of biodiversity:

— It threatens our food supplies, opportunities for recreation and tourism, and sources of wood, medicines and energy.

— It interferes with essential ecological functions such as species balance, soil formation, and greenhouse gas absorption.

— It reduces the productivity of ecosystems, thereby shrinking nature's basket of goods and services, from which we constantly draw.

— It destabilizes ecosystems and weakens their ability to deal with natural disasters such as floods, droughts, and hurricanes, and with human-caused stresses, such as pollution and climate change.

Tourism, especially nature tourism, is closely linked to biodiversity and the attractions created by a rich and varied environment. It can also cause loss of biodiversity when land and resources are strained by excessive use, and when impacts on vegetation, wildlife, mountain, marine and coastal environments and water resources exceed the carrying capacity. This loss of biodiversity in fact means loss of tourism potential.

Tourists and suppliers - often unwittingly - can bring in species (insects, wild and cultivated plants and diseases) that are not native to the local environment and that can cause enormous disruption and even destruction of ecosystems. Tourism means disturbance to the local way of life and disturbance of social structures, and can adversely affect traditional practices that contribute to the conservation and sustainable use of biodiversity. Adverse impacts on livelihoods and lack of benefit sharing with those who bear tourism related costs to both the human and natural environment. Resource use conflicts: competition between tourism and local populations for limited resources of water, sanitation and energy, competition with traditional land uses, especially in heavily used areas such as coastal zones.

Depletiion of Ozone Layer

The ozone layer, which is situated in the upper atmosphere (or stratosphere) at an altitude of 12-50 kilometers, protects life on earth by absorbing the harmful wavelengths of the sun's ultraviolet (UV) radiation, which in high doses is dangerous to humans and animals. For instance, one of the reasons scientists have put forward for the global decrease of amphibian populations is increased exposure to UV radiation.

Ozone depleting substances (ODSs) such as CFCs (chlorofluorocarbon) and halons have contributed to the destruction of this layer. The tourism industry may be part of the problem; direct impacts start with the construction of new developments and continue during daily management and operations. Refrigerators, air conditioners and propellants in aerosol spray cans, amongst others, contain ODSs and are widely used in the hotel and tourism industry. Emissions from jet aircraft are also a significant source of ODSs. According to Tourism Concern, scientists predict that by 2015 half of the annual destruction of the ozone layer will be caused by air travel.

UNEP's Ozon Action Programme works with governments and industries, including the tourism industry, to phase out ODSs and find safer alternatives. UNEP has developed extensive information and guidance on how many types of businesses can eliminate ODSs and contribute to preservation of the ozone layer.

Climate Change

Climate scientists now generally agree that the Earth's surface temperatures have risen steadily in recent years because of an increase in the so-called greenhouse gases in the atmosphere, which trap heat from the sun. One of the most significant of these gases is carbon dioxide (CO_2), which is generated when fossil fuels, such as coal, oil and natural gas are burned (e.g. in industry, electricity generation, and automobiles) and when there are changes in land use, such as deforestation. In the long run, the accumulation of CO_2 and other greenhouse gases in the atmosphere can cause global climate change - a process that may already be occurring.

Global tourism is closely linked to climate change. Tourism involves the movement of people from their homes to other destinations and accounts for about 50% of traffic movements; rapidly expanding air traffic contributes about 2.5% of the production of CO_2. Tourism is thus a significant contributor to the increasing concentrations of greenhouse gases in the atmosphere.

Air travel itself is a major contributor to the greenhouse effect. Passenger jets are the fastest growing source of greenhouse gas emissions. The number of international travelers is expected to increase from 594 million in 1996 to 1.6 billion by 2020, adding greatly to the problem unless steps are taken to reduce emissions.

Environmental Threats to Tourism

Among major threats to tourism due to environmental degradation are: global warming which threatens tourism in coastal areas and small island developing states, in ski resorts, where snow conditions are less reliable; and by other impacts on important resources for recreation and tourism. Recent catastrophes caused by Hurricane Mitch in 1998 affect tourism as much as other sectors of the economy: in 1989 the cost of Hurricane Hugo to the tourism industry in lost revenue alone, was estimated at US$ 8 billion loss of biodiversity linked to human activities and loss of landscape attractiveness affect a number of tourist destinations. For example, in the Mediterranean over 500 plant species are threatened with extinction and tourism has decreased in some overbuilt destinations water pollution damages tourism sites in many regions as well as contaminating the freshwater supply. Lack of freshwater will be more and more, a constraint for tourism development. local air pollution linked to urban congestion can discourage tourists from visiting some destinations.

Natural Disasters

Catastrophes like floods, earthquakes, wildfires, volcanoes, avalanches, drought and diseases can have a serious effect on inbound and domestic tourism and thus on local tourism industries. The outbreak of the foot and mouth disease epidemic in England earlier this year (2001), for instance, has severely affected Great Britain's inbound tourism market. A BHA/Barclays Hospitality Business Trends Survey found that 75% of hotels in England, 81% in Scotland and 85% in Wales continued to be affected by the foot and mouth outbreak, and over 60% forecast a decline in business in the June-September 2001 period.

Climate Change

Tourism not only contributes to climate change, but is affected by it as well. Climate change is likely to increase the severity and frequency of storms and severe weather events, which can have disastrous effects on tourism in the affected regions. Some of the other impacts that the world risks as a result of global warming are drought, diseases and heat waves.

These negative impacts can keep tourists away from the holiday destinations. Global warming may cause:

— Less snowfall at ski resorts, meaning a shorter skiing seasons in the Alpine region. In already hot areas like Asia and the Mediterranean, tourists will stay away because of immense heat, and out of fear of diseases and water shortages.

— Harm to vulnerable ecosystems such as rainforests and coral reefs because of rising temperatures and less rainfall. A major risk to coral reefs is bleaching, which occurs when coral is stressed by temperature increases, high or low levels of salinity, lower water quality, and an increase in suspended sediments. These conditions cause the zooxanthallae (the single-celled algae which forms the colors within the coral) to leave the coral. Without the algae, the coral appears white, or "bleached" - and rapidly dies. The Great Barrier Reef, which supports a US$ 640 million tourism industry, has been experiencing coral bleaching events for the last 20 years.

— Rising sea levels, the result of melting glaciers and polar ice. Higher sea levels will threaten coastal and marine areas with widespread floods in low-lying countries and island states, increasing the loss of coastal land. Beaches and islands that are major tourism attractions may be the first areas to be affected.

— Increased events of extreme weather, such as tornadoes, hurricanes and typhoons. These are already becoming more prevalent in tourist areas in the Caribbean and South East Asia. Hurricane Mitch in 1998, for instance, heavily affected tourism in the Caribbean. Wind damage, storm waves, heavy rains and flooding caused major losses in the local tourism sector.

Effects of Other industries on Tourism

Impacts from other industries often have a more dramatic effect on the environment and can seriously affect tourism.

— Oil spills, like the oil tanker disaster that occurred off the Galapagos Islands (Ecuador) in January 2001, can cause severe short-term damage to tourist attractions. In that case, a freight ship loaded with 160,000 gallons of diesel fuel and 80,000 gallons of other petroleum products ran aground on the coast of San Cristóbal and spilled nearly all of its load. Unique local marine and land species and the tourism potential of the area were badly affected.

— Agricultural runoff or industrial discharges can cause water pollution and may cause algae blooms like those that occurred in the Adriatic Sea in the early 1990s. In spite of improved control of sewage from tourism developments, the Mediterranean sea floor is increasingly carpeted with these quick-growing invaders, many rising 30 inches or more above anchoring runners. They appear equally adept at colonizing rock, mud, and sand in a virtually continuous swath that can extend from the beach out to a depth of about 150 feet, smothering coral reefs, fish and other sea flora and fauna in the process.

— Destructive practices such as blast fishing, fishing with poisonous chemicals like cyanide, and muro-ami netting directly destroy corals. They can also destroy a major draw for tourists.

Tourism Contribution to Environmental Conservation

Tourism can contribute to environmental protection, the conservation of biodiversity, the sustainable use of natural resources and provide much needed resources.

The tourism industry can contribute to conservation through:

FinancialContributions

Direct financial contributions: Tourism can contribute directly to the conservation of sensitive areas and habitat.

Revenue from park-entrance fees and similar sources can be allocated specifically to pay for the protection and management of environmentally sensitive areas. Special fees for park operations or conservation activities can be collected from tourists or tour operators.

The Bonaire Marine Park in the Dutch Antilles was one of the first protected marine areas in the Caribbean to have become entirely self-financing through levying of admission fees on scuba divers. Fees support on-going active management of the park's coral reef, sea grass and mangrove ecosystems, as well as educational activities and orientation sessions for divers, who are the largest user group in the park. The system has been an unqualified success since it was introduced in 1992. In France a tax on marine public transport to some listed protected areas was created in 1995. The aim of this tax, based on the number of passengers, is to provide additional resources for better managing these protected areas, often on islands, which are under pressure from tourism.

The Seychelles in the Indian Ocean is introducing a US$90 tax on travellers entering the Seychelles. Revenue will be used to preserve the environment and improve tourism facilities.

The tourism industry can contribute to the conservation of areas that are assets for their development: parks, protected areas, cultural and natural sites, through financial contributions, provision of environmental infrastructure and improved management. Financial contributions are being made for a limited number of initiatives by the tourism industry and this trend should be further developed.

Tourism also helps raise awareness of the local population with regards to the financial value of natural and cultural sites, makes them proud of this heritage and allies for its conservation. More widely, the involvement of local communities in tourism development and operation appears to be one important condition for the conservation and sustainable use of biodiversity.

This possible contribution of tourism to conservation is one of the reasons explaining the current interest given to the development of nature tourism. However, for sustainable tourism, there is a need to better understand not only the benefits but also the costs of tourism. There is also a need to develop both a more systematic analysis of direct and indirect costs and benefits from tourism as well as green accounting approaches. However, all types of tourism should fully integrate environmental and social considerations. The current focus on nature tourism should not obscure the major challenge to also make mass tourism sustainable.

Contributions to government revenues: Some governments collect money in more far-reaching and indirect ways that are not linked to specific parks or conservation areas. User fees, income taxes, taxes on sales or rental of recreation equipment, and license fees for activities such as hunting and fishing can provide governments with the funds needed to manage natural resources. Such funds can be used for overall conservation programs and activities, such as park ranger salaries and park maintenance.

For Costa Rica, for example, tourism represents 72% of national monetary reserves, generates 140,000 jobs and produces 8.4% of the gross domestic product. The country has 25% of its territory classified under some category of conservation management. In 1999, protected areas welcomed 866,083 national and foreign tourists, who generated about US$ 2.5 million in admission fees and payment of services.

Environmental Management and Planning

Sound environmental management of tourism facilities and especially hotels can increase the benefits to natural areas. But this requires careful planning for controlled development, based on analysis of the environmental resources of the area. Planning helps to make choices between conflicting uses, or to find ways to make them compatible. By planning early for tourism development, damaging and expensive mistakes can be prevented, avoiding the gradual deterioration of environmental assets significant to tourism.

Cleaner production techniques can be important tools for planning and operating tourism facilities in a way that minimizes their environmental impacts. For example, green building (using energy-efficient and non-polluting construction materials, sewage systems and energy sources) is an increasingly important way for the tourism industry to decrease its impact on the environment. And because waste treatment and disposal are often major, long-term environmental problems in the tourism industry, pollution prevention and waste minimization techniques are especially important for the tourism industry. A guide to sources of information on cleaner production (free) is available here.

Environmental Awareness raising

Tourism has the potential to increase public appreciation of the environment and to spread awareness of environmental problems when it brings people into closer contact with nature and the environment. This confrontation may heighten awareness of the value of nature and lead to environmentally conscious behavior and activities to preserve the environment. For instance, Honduran schoolchildren from the capital city of Tegucigalpa are routinely taken to visit La Tigra cloud forest visitor center, funded in part by eco-tourist dollars, to learn about the intricacies of the rainforest.

If it is to be sustainable in the long run, tourism must incorporate the principles and practices of sustainable consumption. Sustainable consumption includes building consumer demand for products that have been made using cleaner production techniques, and for services - including tourism services - that are provided in a way that minimizes environmental impacts. The tourism industry can play a key role in providing environmental information and raising awareness among tourists of the environmental consequences of their actions. Tourists and tourism-related businesses consume an enormous quantity of goods and services; moving them toward using those that are produced and provided in an environmentally sustainable way, from cradle to grave, could have an enormous positive impact on the planet's environment.

Protection and preservation

Tourism can significantly contribute to environmental protection, conservation and restoration of biological diversity and sustainable use of natural resources. Because of their attractiveness, pristine sites and natural areas are identified as valuable and the need to keep the attraction alive can lead to creation of national parks and wildlife parks.

In Hawaii, new laws and regulations have been enacted to preserve the Hawaiian rainforest and to protect native species. The coral reefs around the islands and the marine life that depend on them for survival are also protected. Hawaii now has become an international center for research on ecological systems - and the promotion and preservation of the islands' tourism industry was the main motivation for these actions.

Grupo Punta Cana, a resort in the Dominican Republic, offers an example of how luxury tourism development and conservation can be combined. The high-end resort was established with the goal of catering to luxury-class tourists while respecting the natural habitat of Punta Cana. The developers have set aside 10,000 hectares (24,700 acres) of land as a nature reserve and native fruit tree garden. The Punta Cana Nature Reserve includes 11 fresh water springs surrounded by a subtropical forest where many species of unusual Caribbean flora and fauna live in their natural state. Guests can explore a "nature path" leading from the beach through mangroves, lagoons of fresh water springs and dozens of species of Caribbean bird and plant life.

The Punta Cana Ecological Foundation has begun reforesting some parts of the reserve that had been stripped of their native mahogany and other trees in the past. Other environmentally protective policies have been put into effect at the resort, such as programs to protect the offshore barrier reefs and the recycling of wastewater for use in irrigating the grounds. The fairways of the resort's new golf course were planted with a hybrid grass that can be irrigated with sea water The grass also requires less than half the usual amounts of fertilizer and pesticides. The resort has also established a biodiversity laboratory run by Cornell University.

Tourism has had a positive effect on wildlife preservation and protection efforts, notably in Africa but also in South America, Asia, Australia, and the South Pacific. Numerous animal and plant species have already become extinct or may become extinct soon. Many countries have therefore established wildlife reserves and enacted strict laws protecting the animals that draw nature-loving tourists. As a result of these measures, several endangered species have begun to thrive again.

Alternative Employment

Tourism can provide an alternative to development scenarios that may have greater environmental impacts. The Eco-escuela de Español, a Spanish language school created in 1996 as part of a Conservation International project in the Guatemalan village of San Andres, is an example. The community-owned school, located in the Maya Biosphere Reserve, combines individual language courses with home stay opportunities and community-led eco-tours. It receives around 1,800 tourists yearly, mostly from the US and Europe, and employs almost 100 residents, of whom around 60% were previously engaged in mostly illegal timber extraction, hunting and milpas, or slash-and-burn agriculture. Careful monitoring in 2000 has shown that, among the families benefiting from the business, the majority has significantly reduced hunting practices, and the number and extension of "slash-and-burn" agricultural plots. Furthermore, as most families in the village benefit directly or indirectly from the school, community-managed private reserves have been established, and social pressure against hunting has increased.

Regulatory measures

Regulatory measures help offset negative impacts; for instance, controls on the number of tourist activities and movement of visitors within protected areas can limit impacts on the ecosystem and help maintain the integrity and vitality of the site. Such limits can also reduce the negative impacts on resources. Limits should be established after an in-depth analysis of the maximum sustainable visitor capacity. This strategy is being used in the Galapagos Islands, where the number of ships allowed to cruise this remote archipelago is limited, and only designated islands can be visited, ensuring visitors have little impact on the sensitive environment and animal habitats.

Remaining Challenges

The tourism industry has developed a number of voluntary initiatives for addressing environmental issues: environmental management of tourism facilities and especially hotels is being widely promoted, and progress is being made, particularly for larger hotels, in waste reduction handling, management and disposal, energy and water consumption. This has been promoted by main international industry associations. Numerous industry associations at the regional and national levels have also promoted it.

UNEP has taken part in these efforts. A few tour operators also have implemented environmental programmes and raised environmental awareness of their clients. a number of environmental codes of conduct have also been developed by the tourism sector as well as Action Plans (example of the Caribbean Action for Sustainable Tourism) the tourism industry is also increasingly interested in ecolabels as a means of promoting their facilities and destinations. However, efforts up to now have been concentrated on measures which result in short term economic benefits and there are still many major problems to be solved to put the tourism industry on the path towards sustainability.

The key remaining challenges are to:

— promote wider implementation of environmental management, particularly in the many small and medium enterprises that form the backbone of the tourism industry, and spread initiatives to all sectors of the tourism industry

— use more widely environmentally-sound technologies, in particular to reduce emissions of CO_2 and other greenhouse gases and ozone depleting substances as set out in international agreements

— raise the awareness of tourism clients of the environment and social implications of their holidays, and of opportunities for their responsible behaviour

— develop a better dialogue with the local communities in travel destinations and promote the involvement of local stakeholders in tourism ventures

— work with governments and other stakeholders to improve the overall environmental quality of destinations

— report publicly on environmental performances

— address the key issues of siting and more ecoefficient design of tourism facilities For the tourism industry to remain credible in their commitment to sustainable development, it needs to address the above issues.

Challenges to Governments

A number of initiatives have been taken by governments, in all parts of the world to:

— develop national strategies or master plans for sustainable development of tourism

— develop appropriate regulatory mechanisms and tools such as, environmental assessment,

— development of building regulations and of environmental standards for tourism

— create terrestrial and marine protected areas

— support voluntary initiatives by the tourism industry

However, in many countries the coastline is being overbuilt due to tourism development.

Unfortunately, the same errors are being repeated.

Too often, action is delayed until loss of revenue and cultural and environmental degradation has occurred.

The damage can be irreversible. To achieve sustainable tourism preventative approaches must be adopted.

Facts and figures demonstrate the need for urgent action to avoid irreversible damage from tourism, particularly in coastal and mountain areas.

1. Further Develop and Implement the Legislative and Policy Framework

— ratify, if not already done, and work toward continued implementation of international and regional environmental conventions

— integrate more fully tourism development into the overall plans for sustainable development and

— develop participatory approaches develop more widely land use planning, and protect the coastline through building restrictions

— identify and adopt the most appropriate mix of regulation and economic instruments and, in many cases, develop economic instruments to address environmental issues

— work towards the real enforcement of regulations and standards.

2. Raise Awareness, Build Capacity and Promote Effective Action for Sustainable Tourism

— improve the understanding of the benefits and burdens of tourism in environmental, social

— and economic terms, for the areas under their jurisdiction

— strengthen capacity for the management and control of tourism in their sphere of

— responsibility, and establish and maintain procedures for cooperation and coordination with

— neighbouring authorities, and with relevant state authorities

— provide support through pilot projects and capacity development programmes, including

— capacity development at local government level

— ensure the participation of all stakeholders affected by or involved in tourism and its

— development, especially indigenous and local communities

— ensure that tourism makes a positive contribution to economic development and that the

— economic benefits of tourism are equitably shared

— encourage and catalyse industry initiatives for sustainable tourism across all sectors of the

— tourism, including accommodation, land, air and sea transportation, tour operators, travel agents, attractions sectors, etc.

— promote changes in consumer behaviour in both tourist originating countries and destinations towards more sustainable forms of tourism

15. Develop Monitoring of Progress towards Sustainable Tourism develop activities to monitor, control and mitigate adverse effects that may arise from tourism activities and development.

Challenges to NGOs

Many NGOs have already made significant steps in modifying consumers' preferences and behaviour, making sensitive issues public and highlighting problematic areas and thus influencing decisions. They have also increased the environmental awareness and educational level with great positive results. An example among others is the "Blue Flag" campaign, conducted by the Foundation for Environmental Education in Europe, which contributed to the improvement in the quality of European beaches and marinas.

The remaining challenges are given below:

— more specifically voice their views in tourism policies and strategies

— contribute to development, and implementation, of environmental standards for tourism

— develop or participate in raising awareness and education activities for sensitising tourists towards improving guest consumption patterns

— assist with monitoring tourism activities and development and progress towards more sustainable tourism.

Challenges to International Community

Many international organisations have, in line with their mission and field of expertise, developed programmes and activities to help put tourism on the path towards sustainability.

The World Tourism Organisation has also been active focusing in particular on planning at the national and local levels and on indicators for sustainable tourism and in addressing sustainable tourism in a number of regional events.

A number of other international organizations have developed activities for sustainable tourism and, in particular, UNESCO: tourism in World Heritage Sites, cultural tourism etc.

Many regional organisations and in particular the various UN Economic and Social Commissions have also developed activities to support sustainable tourism in their region

To help catalyse appropriate action UNEP has recently proposed "Principles for Implementation of Sustainable Tourism". The Principles are being designed to provide a coherent framework for more specific guidelines to be prepared by the various Conventions: Biological Diversity, Climate Change, Regional Seas Action Plans, and other international agreements, that have already or will address tourism issues; and to help Governments, intergovernmental, private-sector and other organisations in applying the general concept of sustainable tourism in practice.

The key remaining challenges are to:

— assist and support governments in development of national strategies or master plans for sustainable development of tourism and of environmental land use and building regulations and standards for tourism

— raise awareness and build capacity of all stakeholders by providing information on best practices for sustainable tourism

— encourage the private sector to develop and apply codes and guidelines, environmental management systems, and promote the development of the use of environmental reporting by companies in the various branches of the tourism sector

— assist in assessing the environmental effectiveness of existing voluntary initiatives in the various branches of the tourism sector and present corresponding recommendations

— promote the transfer of Environmentally Sound Technologies (ESTs), practices, and management tools adapted for the tourism sector, and disseminate information on ESTs to governments and the tourism industry

— work with other stakeholders to establish, and disseminate lessons from, Best Practices projects on sustainable tourism

— provide support through provision of information and capacity development programmes particularly on the costs and benefits of tourism development, the use of economic incentives to promote sustainable tourism, and on destination management assist in establishment of monitoring of progress towards sustainable tourism.

Emerging Issues

— *Developing partnership:* For sustainable tourism the involvement and commitment of all stakeholders are essential. However, public, private and academic sector partnerships are still underdeveloped and therefore need to be encouraged.

— *Involvement of the banking and insurance sectors:* banks and insurance companies could greatly expedite progress of sustainable tourism by incorporating environmental and social criteria into assessment procedures for loans, investments, and insurance. They could help finance environmentally-sound technologies and provide incentives for sustainable tourism. This approach has worked well in other contexts. Widespread involvement of the banking and insurance sectors should be sought.

— *Use of economic instruments*: the tourism industry consumes increasingly scarce natural resources. The costing of energy and water in particular could expedite greatly ecoefficiency in the tourism industry and raise revenue for the improved management of these resources. Governments should consider the development and widespread use of economic instruments for sustainable tourism.

— *Involvement of tourism boards:* Often, marketing strategies and messages are not in line with the principles of sustainable tourism. There is the need to better . involve tourism boards in sustainable tourism efforts.

— *Capacity building of local government:* In many countries, local governments have important responsibilities regarding tourism development. Capacity building programmes should be implemented to help them understand these responsibilities, develop integrated and participatory approaches and define and implement policies for sustainable tourism.

— *Greater focus on transport:* There is a continued development of long-haul travel. Economic, technological and management approaches should be developed to reduce emissions, waste and pollution resulting from tourism transportation. Changing consumption patterns should also be considered.

— *Emerging types of tourism:* Tourism is rapidly diversifying. Emerging forms of tourism should also develop according to sustainability criteria. Currently, the increase of cruises and the current trend towards mega-ships, necessitate that the cruise ship industry develops a socially and environmentally responsible approach.

— *Improve monitoring*: Careful monitoring of impacts and results as well as the adoption of corrective measures are conditions for sustainable tourism. All stakeholders at all levels should thus develop monitoring. As previously stated, the private sector should develop monitoring and public reporting of their activities.

> Local and central governments should develop, more widely, monitoring tools such as indicators, and incorporate the results into their decision making process. Where appropriate, participatory approaches should be used. Monitoring is currently uncommon and this should be a priority.

3

Socio-economic Impacts

Tourism is the temporary movement of people to destinations outside their normal places of work and residence, the activities undertaken during their stay in those destinations, and the facilities created to cater to their needs. During their stay in the destination, tourists interact with local residents and the outcome of their relationship is changes in the host individuals' and host community's quality of life, value systems, labour division, family relationships, attitudes, behavioural patterns, ceremonies and creative expressions. The larger the cultural and economic difference between tourists and local residents, the more obvious and more significant these changes are.

Changes in the host community's quality of life are influenced by two major factors: the tourist-host relationship and the development of the industry itself.

Tourist-host encounters occur in three main contexts:

— where the tourist is buying some good or service from the host,

— where they are in the same place at the same time, and

— when they meet and share ideas and information

As the last type of encounter is far less common than the first two, tourism often fails in promoting mutual understanding among different nations and stereotypes prevail.

The tourist-host relationship is characterised by four major features: it is transitory, unequal and unbalanced, lacks spontaneity and is limited by spatial and temporal constraints. The tourist usually stays in the destination for a short time, so there is no opportunity to develop the superficial relationship into a more meaningful one. The traditional spontaneous hospitality turns into commercial activity. Tourists are on holiday, served by locals, which results in different attitudes and behaviour. The obvious relative wealth of the tourists often leads to exploitative behaviour on the hosts' side.

The main impacts affected by the tourist-host relationship are the demonstration effect, when the hosts' behaviour is modified in order to imitate tourists; the change in language usage in the destination; the growth of alcoholism, crime, prostitution and gambling and the transformation (revitalisation or commoditisation) of the material and non-material forms of local culture.

Besides the physical presence of tourists and their encounters with local residents, the development of the tourism industry also contributes to changes in the quality of life, social structure and social organisation of local residents. Rapid and intensive tourism development results in different and usually less favourable impacts than organic and small-scale development.

The development of the tourism industry is often credited for generating new employment in the destination. However, much of this employment is seasonal, unskilled and low-paid, and the community's traditional work patterns might be seriously affected, resulting in the abandonment of agricultural occupations.

Other significant impacts of tourism development are changes in the size and the demographic characteristics of the host population; alteration of community structure; increased mobility of women and young adults; infrastructural development in the destination, increased supply of services, and, consequently, improved quality of life for local residents.

The social and cultural characteristics of the host community are, of course, also continuously influenced by the political, economic, technological, social, cultural and natural aspects of their wider environment. The problem of separating tourism's impacts from these influences is unsolved yet, so this research only deals with impacts perceived by residents as the impacts of tourism development.

The main objective of socio-cultural impact analysis is to provide developers, local authorities and all other parties concerned with information on the host communities' perceptions of and attitudes to tourism development in their destination, so that perceived positive impacts could be reinforced and perceived negative impacts could be minimised.

Apart from obvious and visible effects on the economy and the physical environment, tourism can contribute to social and cultural changes in host societies, including changes in value systems, traditional lifestyles, family relationships, individual behaviour or community structure. The socio-cultural impacts of tourism described here are the effects on host communities of direct and indirect relations with tourists, and of interaction with the tourism industry. For a variety of reasons, host communities often are the weaker party in interactions with their guests and service providers, leveraging any influence they might have. These influences are not always apparent, as they are difficult to measure, depend on value judgments and are often indirect or hard to identify.

The impacts arise when tourism brings about changes in value systems and behaviour and thereby threatens indigenous identity. Furthermore, changes often occur in community structure, family relationships, collective traditional life styles, ceremonies and morality. But tourism can also generate positive impacts as it can serve as a supportive force for peace, foster pride in cultural traditions and help avoid urban relocation by creating local jobs. As often happens when different cultures meet, socio-cultural impacts are ambiguous: the same objectively described impacts are seen as beneficial by some groups, and are perceived as negative - or as having negative aspects - by other stakeholders.

Negative Socio-cultural Impacts

Change or Loss of Indigenous Identity and Values

Tourism can cause change or loss of local identity and values, brought about by several closely related influences:

Commodification

Tourism can turn local cultures into commodities when religious rituals, traditional ethnic rites and festivals are reduced and sanitized to conform to tourist expectations, resulting in what has been called "reconstructed ethnicity." Once a destination is sold as a tourism product, and the tourism demand for souvenirs, arts, entertainment and other commodities begins to exert influence, basic changes in human values may occur. Sacred sites and objects may not be respected when they are perceived as goods to trade.

Standardization

Destinations risk standardization in the process of satisfying tourists' desires for familiar facilities. While landscape, accommodation, food and drinks, etc., must meet the tourists' desire for the new and unfamiliar, they must at the same time not be too new or strange because few tourists are actually looking for completely new things. Tourists often look for recognizable facilities in an unfamiliar environment, like well-known fast-food restaurants and hotel chains.

Loss of authenticity and staged authenticity

Adapting cultural expressions and manifestations to the tastes of tourists or even performing shows as if they were "real life" constitutes "staged authenticity". As long as tourists just want a glimpse of the local atmosphere, a quick glance at local life, without any knowledge or even interest, staging will be inevitable.

Adaptation to tourist demands

Tourists want souvenirs, arts, crafts, and cultural manifestations, and in many tourist destinations, craftsmen have responded to the growing demand, and have made changes in design of their products to bring them more in line with the new customers' tastes. While the interest shown by tourists also contributes to the sense of self-worth of the artists, and helps conserve a cultural tradition, cultural erosion may occur due to the commodification of cultural goods.

Culture Clashes

Because tourism involves movement of people to different geographical locations, and establishment of social relations between people who would otherwise not meet, cultural clashes can take place as a result of differences in cultures, ethnic and religious groups, values and lifestyles, languages, and levels of prosperity.

The result can be an overexploitation of the social carrying capacity (limits of acceptable change in the social system inside or around the destination) and cultural carrying capacity (limits of acceptable change in the culture of the host population) of the local community.

The attitude of local residents towards tourism development may unfold through the stages of euphoria, where visitors are very welcome, through apathy, irritation and potentially antagonism, when anti-tourist attitudes begin growing among local people.

Cultural clashes may further arise through:

Economic inequality

Many tourists come from societies with different consumption patterns and lifestyles than what is current at the destination, seeking pleasure, spending large amounts of money and sometimes behaving in ways that even they would not accept at home. One effect is that local people that come in contact with these tourists may develop a sort of copying behavior, as they want to live and behave in the same way.

Especially in less developed countries, there is likely to be a growing distinction between the 'haves' and 'have-nots', which may increase social and sometimes ethnic tensions. In resorts in destination countries such as Jamaica, Indonesia or Brazil, tourism employees with average yearly salaries of US$ 1,200 to 3,000 spend their working hours in close contact with guests whose yearly income is well over US$ 80,000.

Irritation due to tourist behavior

Tourists often, out of ignorance or carelessness, fail to respect local customs and moral values. When they do, they can bring about irritation and stereotyping. They take a quick snapshot and are gone, and by so acting invade the local peoples' lives.

In many Muslim countries, strict standards exist regarding the appearance and behaviour of Muslim women, who must carefully cover themselves in public. Tourists in these countries often disregard or are unaware of these standards, ignoring the prevalent dress code, appearing half-dressed (by local standards) in revealing shorts, skirts or even bikinis, sunbathing topless at the beach or consuming large quantities of alcohol openly. Besides creating ill-will, this kind of behavior can be an incentive for locals not to respect their own traditions and religion anymore, leading to tensions within the local community. The same types of culture clashes happen in conservative Christian communities in Polynesia, the Caribbean and the Mediterranean.

Job level friction

In developing countries especially, many jobs occupied by local people in the tourist industry are at a lower level, such as housemaids, waiters, gardeners and other practical work, while higher-paying and more prestigious managerial jobs go to foreigners or "urbanized" nationals. Due to a lack of professional training, as well as to the influence of hotel or restaurant chains at the destination, people with the know-how needed to perform higher level jobs are often attracted from other countries. This may cause friction and irritation and increases the gap between the cultures.

Even in cases where tourism "works", in the sense that it improves local economies and the earning power of local individuals, it cannot solve all local social or economic problems. Sometimes it substitutes new problems for old ones.

Physical Influences Causing Social Stress

The physical influences that the increasing tourism flow, and its consequent developments, have on a destination can cause severe social stress as it impacts the local community. Socio-cultural disadvantages evolve from:

— Resource use conflicts, such as competition between tourism and local populations for the use of prime resources like water and energy because of scarce supply. Stress to local communities can also result from environmental degradation and increased infrastructure costs for the local community - for example, higher taxes to pay for improvements to the water supply or sanitation facilities.

— Cultural deterioration. Damage to cultural resources may arise from vandalism, littering, pilferage and illegal removal of cultural heritage items. A common problem at archaeological sites in countries such as Egypt, Colombia, Mexico and Peru is that poorly paid guards supplement their income by selling artifacts to tourists. Furthermore, degradation of cultural sites may occur when historic sites and buildings are unprotected and the traditionally built environment is replaced or virtually disappears.

— Conflicts with traditional land-uses, especially in intensely exploited areas such as coastal zones, which are popular for their beaches and islands. Conflicts arise when the choice has to be made between development of the land for tourist facilities or infrastructure and local traditional land-use. The indigenous population of such destinations is frequently the loser in the contest for these resources as the economic value which tourism brings often counts for more.

As an example of how local people can suffer from tourism development, in coastal areas construction of shoreline hotels and tourist faculties often cuts off access for the locals to traditional fishing ground and even recreational use of the areas.

Ethical Issues

Partly due to the above impacts, tourism can create more serious situations where ethical and even criminal issues are involved.

Crime generation

Crime rates typically increase with the growth and urbanization of an area, and growth of mass tourism is often accompanied by increased crime. The presence of a large number of tourists with a lot of money to spend, and often carrying valuables such as cameras and jewelry, increases the attraction for criminals and brings with it activities like robbery and drug dealing. Repression of these phenomena often exacerbates social tension. In Rio de Janeiro, Brazil, tourists staying in beachside five star resorts close to extremely poor communities in hillside "favelas" (shantytowns) are at risk of pickpockets and stick-ups. Security agents, often armed with machine guns, stand guard nearby in full sight, and face aggressive reactions from locals who are often their neighbors when they go home. Tourism can also drive the development of gambling, which may cause negative changes in social behavior.

Child labour

ILO studies show that many jobs in the tourism sector have working and employment conditions that leave much to be desired: long hours, unstable employment, low pay, little training and poor chances for qualification. In addition, recent developments in the travel and tourism trade (liberalization, competition, concentration, drop in travel fares, growth of subcontracting) and introduction of new technologies seem to reinforce the trend towards more precarious, flexible employment conditions. For many such jobs young children are recruited, as they are cheap and flexible employees.

An estimated 13-19 million children and young people below 18 years of age (10-15 per cent of all employees in tourism) are employed in the industry worldwide. However, these figures take no account of the number of children working in the informal sector in ancillary activities. Child labour in tourism is common in both developing and in developed countries. Many boys and girls below 12 years of age are engaged in small business activities related to hotels and restaurants, the entertainment sector or the souvenir trade, often as porters or street or beach vendors. They are frequently subjected to harsh working and employment conditions. Source: ILO

Prostitution and sex tourism

The commercial sexual exploitation of children and young women has paralleled the growth of tourism in many parts of the world. Though tourism is not the cause of sexual exploitation, it provides easy access to it. Tourism also brings consumerism to many parts of the world previously denied access to luxury commodities and services. The lure of this easy money has caused many young people, including children, to trade their bodies in exchange for T-shirts, personal stereos, bikes and even air tickets out of the country. In other situations children are trafficked into the brothels on the margins of the tourist areas and sold into sex slavery, very rarely earning enough money to escape.

The United Nations has defined child sex tourism as "tourism organized with the primary purpose of facilitating the effecting of a commercial sexual relationship with a child". Certain tourism destinations have become centers for this illegal trade, frequented by paedophiles and supported by networks of pimps, taxi drivers, hotel staff, brothel owners, entertainment establishments, and tour operators who organize package sex tours. At the international level, there are agents who provide information about particular resorts where such practices are commonplace.

Although sexual exploitation of children is a worldwide phenomenon, it is more prevalent in Asia than elsewhere. ECPAT, an organization that fights child sex tourism, has started a campaign against child prostitution in Asian tourism. In 2000 ECPAT international created a Certified Code of Conduct (CCC) for tour operators against child sex tourism and this year initiated a follow-up project, the "Code of Conduct of the Tourism Industry to protect children from sexual exploitation".

Role of Tourism in Socio-cultural Development

Tourism can contribute to positive developments, not just negative impacts. It has the potential to promote social development through employment creation, income redistribution and poverty alleviation. Other potential positive impacts of tourism include:

Tourism as a Force for Peace

Traveling brings people into contact with each other and, as tourism has an educational element, it can foster understanding between peoples and cultures and provide cultural exchange between hosts and guests. Because of this, the chances increase for people to develop mutual sympathy and understanding and to reduce their prejudices. For example, jobs provided by tourism in Belfast, Northern Ireland, are expected to help demobilize paramilitary groups as the peace process is put in place. In the end, sympathy and understanding can lead to a decrease of tension in the world and thus contribute to peace.

Strengthening Communities

Tourism can add to the vitality of communities in many ways. One example is that events and festivals of which local residents have been the primary participants and spectators are often rejuvenated and developed in response to tourist interest.

The jobs created by tourism can act as a vital incentive to reduce emigration from rural areas. Local people can also increase their influence on tourism development, as well as improve their job and earnings prospects, through tourism-related professional training and development of business and organizational skills.

The San of Namibia and southern Africa and the aboriginal peoples of Australia have recently regained management or ownership of traditional national park lands and conservancies, operating ecolodges and serving as guides and rangers while maintaining their heritage.

Support for Creation of Community Facilities

As tourism supports the creation of community facilities and services that otherwise might not have been developed, it can bring higher living standards to a destination. Benefits can include upgraded infrastructure, health and transport improvements, new sport and recreational facilities, restaurants, and public spaces as well as an influx of better-quality commodities and food.

Revaluation of Culture and Traditions

Tourism can boost the preservation and transmission of cultural and historical traditions, which often contributes to the conservation and sustainable management of natural resources, the protection of local heritage, and a renaissance of indigenous cultures, cultural arts and crafts.

The tour operator Travel Walji's, for example, is complementing conservation efforts not only by providing direct financial assistance, but also by providing indirect support, such as tourism development aid, to a remote mountain destination in the Karakorum region of South Asia. The aid has helped revive local music and traditional activities like sword dancing.

Encouragement to Civic Involvement

Tourism also helps raise local awareness of the financial value of natural and cultural sites and can stimulate a feeling of pride in local and national heritage and interest in its conservation. More broadly, the involvement of local communities in tourism development and operation appears to be an important condition for the conservation and sustainable use of biodiversity.

These are some positive consequences of tourism that can arise only when tourism is practiced and developed in a sustainable and appropriate way. Involving the local population is essential. A community involved in planning and implementation of tourism has a more positive attitude, is more supportive and has a better chance to make a profit from tourism than a population passively ruled - or overrun - by tourism. One of the core elements of sustainable tourism development is community development, which is a process and a capacity to make decisions that consider the long-term economy, ecology and equity of all communities.

Economic Impacts of Tourism

Businesses and public organizations are increasingly interested in the economic impacts of tourism at national, state, and local levels. Tourism supports jobs in an area or that a festival or special event generated million dollars in sales or income in a community. Multiplier effects are often cited to capture secondary effects of tourism spending and show the wide range of sectors in a community that may benefit from tourism.

Tourism's economic benefits are touted by the industry for a variety of reasons. Claims of tourism's economic significance give the industry greater respect among the business community, public officials, and the public in general. This often translates into decisions or public policies that are favorable to tourism. Community support is important for tourism, as it is an activity that affects the entire community.

Tourism businesses depend extensively on each other as well as on other businesses, government and residents of the local community. Economic benefits and costs of tourism reach virtually everyone in the region in one way or another. Economic impact analyses provide tangible estimates of these economic interdependencies and a better understanding of the role and importance of tourism in a region's economy.

Tourism activity also involves economic costs, including the direct costs incurred by tourism businesses, government costs for infrastructure to better serve tourists, as well as congestion and related costs borne by individuals in the community. Community decisions over tourism often involve debates between industry proponents touting tourism's economic impacts (benefits) and detractors emphasizing tourism's costs. Sound decisions rest on a balanced and objective assessment of both benefits and costs and an understanding of who benefits from tourism and who pays for it. Tourism's economic impacts are therefore an important consideration in state, regional and community planning and economic development. Economic impacts are also important factors in marketing and management decisions. Communities therefore need to understand the relative importance of tourism to their region, including tourism's contribution to economic activity in the area.

A variety of methods, ranging from pure guesswork to complex mathematical models, are used to estimate tourism's economic impacts. Studies vary extensively in quality and accuracy, as well as which aspects of tourism are included. Technical reports often are filled with economic terms and methods that non-economists do not understand. On the other hand, media coverage of these studies tend to oversimplify and frequently misinterpret the results, leaving decision makers and the general public with a sometimes distorted and incomplete understanding of tourism's economic effects.

How can the average person understand these studies sufficiently to separate good studies from bad ones and make informed choices? The purpose of this bulletin is to present a systematic introduction to economic impact concepts and methods. The presentation is written for tourism industry analysts and public officials, who would like to better understand, evaluate, or possibly conduct an economic impact assessment. The bulletin is organized around ten basic questions that either are asked or should be asked about the economic impacts of tourism.

Impact Analysis

A variety of economic analyses are carried out to support tourism decisions. As these different kinds of economic analysis are frequently confused, let's begin by positioning economic impact studies within the broader set of economic problems and techniques relevant to tourism. These same techniques may be applied to any policy or action, but we will define them here in the context of tourism. Each type of analysis is identified by the basic question(s) it answers and the types of methods and models that are appropriate.

Benefit cost analysis and economic impact analysis are frequently confused as both discuss economic "benefits". There are two clear distinctions between the two techniques. B/C analysis addresses the benefits from economic efficiency while economic impact analysis focuses on the regional distribution of economic activity. The income received from tourism by a destination region is largely off-set by corresponding losses in the origin regions, yielding only modest contributions to net social welfare and efficiency. B/C analysis includes both market and non-market values (consumer surplus), while economic impact analysis is restricted to actual flows of money from market transactions.

While each type of economic analysis is somewhat distinct, a given problem often calls for several different kinds of economic analysis. An economic impact study will frequently involve a demand analysis to project levels of tourism activity. In other cases demand is treated as exogenous and the analysis simply estimates impacts if a given number of visitors are attracted to the area. A comprehensive impact assessment will also examine fiscal impacts, as well as social and environmental impacts.

Be aware that an economic impact analysis, by itself, provides a rather narrow and often one-sided perspective on the impacts of tourism. Studies of the economic impacts of tourism tend to emphasize the positive benefits of tourism. On the other hand environmental, social, cultural and fiscal impact studies tend to focus more on negative impacts of tourism. This is in spite of the fact that there are negative economic impacts of tourism (e.g., seasonality and lower wage jobs) and in many cases positive environmental and social impacts (e.g., protection of natural & cultural resources in the area and education of both tourists and local residents).

An economic impact assessment (EIA) traces changes in economic activity resulting from some action. An EIA will identify which economic sectors benefit from tourism and estimate resulting changes in income and employment in the region. Economic impact assessment procedures do not assess economic efficiency and also do not generally produce estimates of the fiscal costs of an action. For many problems economic impact analysis will be part of a broader analysis. Environmental, social, and fiscal impacts are often equally important concerns in a balanced assessment of impacts.

An economic impact analysis will assess the contribution of tourism activity to a region's economy. The basic questions an economic impact study usually addresses are:

— How much do tourists spend in the area?

— What portion of sales by local businesses is due to tourism?

— How much income does tourism generate for households and businesses in the area?

— How many jobs in the area does tourism support?

— How much tax revenue is generated from tourism?

An economic impact analysis also reveals the interrelationships among economic sectors and provides estimates of the changes that take place in an economy due to some existing or proposed action. The most common applications of economic impact analysis to tourism are:

— To evaluate the economic impacts of changes in the supply of recreation and tourism opportunities. Supply changes may involve a change in quantity, such as the opening of new facilities, closing of existing ones, or expansions and contraction in capacity. Supply changes may also involve changes in quality, including changes in (a) the quality of the environment, (b) the local infrastructure and public services to support tourism, or (ç) the nature of the tourism products and services that are provided in an area.

— To evaluate the economic impacts of changes in tourism demand. Population changes, changes in the competitive position of the region, marketing activity or changing consumer tastes and preferences can alter levels of tourism activity, spending, and associated economic activity. An economic impact study can estimate the magnitude and nature of these impacts.

— To evaluate the effects of policies and actions which affect tourism activity either directly or indirectly. Tourism depends on many factors at both origins and destinations that are frequently outside the direct control of the tourism industry itself. Economic impact studies provide information to help decision makers better understand the consequences of various actions on the tourism industry as well as on other sectors of the economy. For example, increased air pollution standards have been opposed in some regions due to the predicted economic consequences of the closing of plants that cannot meet the new standards. Tourism interests counter these arguments with estimates of the potential gains in income and jobs in tourism industries that depend on good air quality and visibility.

— To understand the economic structure and interdependencies of different sectors of the economy.

Economic studies help us better understand the size and structure of the tourism industry in a given region and its linkages to other sectors of the economy. Such understandings are helpful in identifying potential partners for the tourism industry as well as in targeting industries as part of regional economic development strategies. Issues such as economic growth, stability, and seasonality may be addressed as part of these studies.

— To argue for favorable treatment in allocation of resources or local tax, zoning or other policy decisions. By showing that tourism has significant economic impacts, tourism interests can often convince decision-makers to allocate more resources for tourism or to establish policies that encourage tourism. Tax abatements and other incentives frequently given to manufacturing firms have also been granted to hotels, marinas and other tourism businesses based on demonstrated economic impacts in the local area.

— To compare the economic impacts of alternative resource allocation, policy, management or development proposals. Economic impact analyses are commonly used to assess the relative merits of distinct alternatives. The economic contribution of expanded tourism offerings may be compared for example with alternatives such as resource extraction activities (mining, timber harvesting) or manufacturing. Impacts of alternative tourism development proposals may also be evaluated, e.g., tourism strategies that emphasize outdoor recreation, camping development, a convention facility, or a factory outlet mall.

Types of Impacts

Tourism has a variety of economic impacts. Tourists contribute to sales, profits, jobs, tax revenues, and income in an area. The most direct effects occur within the primary tourism sectors-lodging, restaurants, transportation, amusements, and retail trade . Through secondary effects, tourism affects most sectors of the economy. An economic impact analysis of tourism activity normally focuses on changes in sales, income, and employment in a region resulting from tourism activity.

A simple tourism impact scenario illustrates. Let's say a region attracts an additional 100 tourists, each spending $100 per day. That's $10,000 in new spending per day in the area. If sustained over a 100 day season, the region would accumulate a million dollars in new sales. The million dollars in spending would be distributed to lodging, restaurant, amusement and retail trade sectors in proportion to how the visitor spends the $100.

Perhaps 30% of the million dollars would leak out of the region immediately to cover the costs of goods purchased by tourists that are not made in the local area (only the retail margins for such items should normally be included as direct sales effects). The remaining $700,000 in direct sales might yield $350,000 in income within tourism industries and support 20 direct tourism jobs. Tourism industries are labor and income intensive, translating a high proportion of sales into income and corresponding jobs.

The tourism industry, in turn, buys goods and services from other businesses in the area, and pays out most of the $350,000 in income as wages and salaries to its employees. This creates secondary economic effects in the region. The study might use a sales multiplier of 2.0 to indicate that each dollar of direct sales generates another dollar in secondary sales in this region. Through multiplier effects, the $700,000 in direct sales produces

$1.4 million in total sales. These secondary sales create additional income and employment, resulting in a total impact on the region of $1.4 million in sales, $650,000 in income and 35 jobs. While hypothetical, the numbers used here are fairly typical of what one might find in a tourism economic impact study.

A more complete study might identify which sectors receive the direct and secondary effects and possibly identify differences in spending and impacts of distinct subgroups of tourists (market segments). One can also estimate the tax effects of this spending by applying local tax rates to the appropriate changes in sales or income. Instead of focusing on visitor spending, one could also estimate impacts of construction or government activity associated with tourism.

There are several other categories of economic impacts that are not typically covered in economic impact assessments, at least not directly. For example:

— Changes in prices-tourism can sometimes inflate the cost of housing and retail prices in the area, frequently on a seasonal basis.

— Changes in the quality and quantity of goods and services - tourism may lead to a wider array of goods and services available in an area (of either higher or lower quality than without tourism).

— Changes in property and other taxes - taxes to cover the cost of local services may be higher or lower in the presence of tourism activity. In some cases, taxes collected directly or indirectly from tourists may yield reduced local taxes for schools, roads, etc. In other cases, locals may be taxed more heavily to cover the added infrastructure and service costs. The impacts of tourism on local government costs and revenues are addressed more fully in a fiscal impact analysis.

— Economic dimensions of "social" and "environmental" impacts - There are also economic consequences of most social and environmental impacts that are not usually addressed in an economic impact analysis. These can be positive or negative. For example, traffic congestion will increase costs of moving around for both households and businesses. Improved amenities that attract tourists may also encourage retirees or other kinds of businesses to locate in the area.

Direct, Indirect and Induced Effects

A standard economic impact analysis traces flows of money from tourism spending, first to businesses and government agencies where tourists spend their money and then to:

— *other businesses*-supplying goods and services to tourist businesses,

— *households* - earning income by working in tourism or supporting industries, and

— *government*-through various taxes and charges on tourists, businesses and households

Formally, regional economists distinguish direct, indirect, and induced economic effects. Indirect and induced effects are sometimes collectively called secondary effects. The total economic impact of tourism is the sum of direct, indirect, and induced effects within a region. Any of these impacts may be measured as gross output or sales, income, employment, or value added.

Direct effects are production changes associated with the immediate effects of changes in tourism expenditures. For example, an increase in the number of tourists staying overnight in hotels would directly yield increased sales in the hotel sector. The additional hotel sales and associated changes in hotel payments for wages and salaries, taxes, and supplies and services are direct effects of the tourist spending.

Indirect effects are the production changes resulting from various rounds of re-spending of the hotel industry's receipts in other backward-linked industries (i.e., industries supplying products and services to hotels). Changes in sales, jobs, and income in the linen supply industry, for example, represent indirect effects of changes in hotel sales. Businesses supplying products and services to the linen supply industry represent another round of indirect effects, eventually linking hotels to varying degrees to many other economic sectors in the region.

Induced effects are the changes in economic activity resulting from household spending of income earned directly or indirectly as a result of tourism spending. For example, hotel and linen supply employees, supported directly or indirectly by tourism, spend their income in the local region for housing, food, transportation, and the usual array of household product and service needs. The sales, income, and jobs that result from household spending of added wage, salary, or proprietor's income are induced effects.

By means of indirect and induced effects, changes in tourist spending can impact virtually every sector of the economy in one way or another. The magnitude of secondary effects depends on the propensity of businesses and households in the region to purchase goods and services from local suppliers. Induced effects are particularly noticed when a large employer in a region closes a plant. Not only are supporting industries (indirect effects) hurt, but the entire local economy suffers due to the reduction in household income within the region. Retail stores close and leakages of money from the region increase as consumers go outside the region for more and more goods and services. Similar effects in the opposite direction are observed when there is a significant increase in jobs and household income.

Final demand is the term used by economists for sales to the final consumers of goods and services. In almost all cases, the final consumers of tourism goods and services are households. Government spending is also considered as final demand. The same methods for estimating impacts of visitor spending can be applied to estimate the economic impacts of government spending, for example, to operate and maintain a park or visitor center.

Regional economic models

An input-output model (I-O model) is a mathematical model that describes the flows of money between sectors within a region's economy. Flows are predicted by knowing what each industry must buy from every other industry to produce a dollar's worth of output. Using each industry's production function, I-O models also determine the proportions of sales that go to wage and salary income, proprietor's income, and taxes. Multipliers can be estimated from input-output models based on the estimated re-circulation of spending within the region.

Exports and imports are determined based upon estimates of the propensity of households and firms within the region to purchase goods and services from local sources. The more a region is self-sufficient and purchases goods and services from within the region, the higher the multipliers for the region.

Input-output models make a number of assumptions. The basic ones are that:

— All firms in a given industry employ the same production technology (usually assumed to be the national average for that industry), and produce identical products.

— There are no economies or diseconomies of scale in production or factor substitution. I-O models are essentially linear-double the level of tourism activity/ production and you double all of the inputs, the number of jobs, etc.

— The model doesn't explicitly keep track of time, but analysts generally report the impact estimates as if they represent activity within a single year.

— One must assume that the various model parameters are accurate and represent the current year. I-O models are firmly grounded in the national system of accounts, which relies on a standard industrial classification system (SIC codes) and various federal government economic censuses, in which individual firms report sales, wage and salary payments and employment. I-O models will generally be at least a few years out-of-date, although this isn't usually a major problem unless the region's economy has changed significantly. An I-O model represents the region's economy at a particular point in time.

— Multiplier computations for induced effects generally assume that jobs created by additional spending are new jobs, involving new households in the area. Induced effects are computed assuming linear changes in household spending with changes in income. Estimates of induced effects may be inflated due to the violation of these assumptions. Induced effects tend to account for the vast majority of the secondary effects of tourism, and therefore should be used with caution.

Multiplier effects

Multipliers capture the secondary economic effects (indirect and induced) of tourism activity. Multipliers have been frequently misused and misinterpreted in tourism studies and are a considerable source of confusion among non-economists. Multipliers represent the economic interdependencies between sectors within a particular region's economy. They vary considerably from region to region and sector to sector. There are many different kinds of multipliers reflecting which secondary effects are included and which measure of economic activity is used (sales, income, or employment).

For example,

$$\text{The Type I sales multiplier} = \frac{\text{direct sales + indirect sales}}{\text{direct sales.}}$$

$$\text{The Type II or III sales multiplier} = \frac{\text{direct sales + indirect sales + induced sales}}{\text{direct sales.}}$$

Multiplying a Type I sales multiplier times the direct sales gives direct plus indirect sales. Multiplying a Type II or III sales multiplier times the direct sales gives total sales impacts including direct, indirect and induced effects. The multipliers defined above are called ratio type multipliers as they measure the ratio of a total impact measure to the corresponding direct impact. Comparable income and employment ratio type multipliers may be defined by replacing sales with measures of income or employment in the above equations. Ratio multipliers should be used with caution.

A common error is to multiply a sales multiplier times tourist spending to get total sales effects. This will generate an inflated estimate of tourism impacts. The problem is that tourism spending or sales is not exactly the same as the "direct effects", appearing in the multiplier formula. Tourist purchases of goods (vs. services) are the primary source of the problem.

To properly apply tourist purchases of goods to an input-output model (or corresponding multipliers), various margins (retail, wholesale and transportation) must be deducted from the "purchaser price" of the good to separate out the "producer price". In an I-O model, retail margins accrue to the retail trade sector, wholesale margins to wholesale trade, transportation margins to transportation sectors (trucking, rail, air etc.) and the producer prices of goods are assigned to the sector that produces the good.

In most cases the factory that produces the good bought by a tourist lies outside of the local region, creating an immediate "leakage" in the first round of spending and therefore no local impact from production of the good. Before applying a multiplier to tourist spending, one must first deduct the producer prices of all imported goods that tourists buy (i.e. only include the local retail margins and possibly wholesale and transportation margins if these firms lie within the region).

Generally, only 60 to 70% of tourist spending appears as final demand in a local region. While all tourist purchases of services will accrue to the local region as final demand , only the margins on goods purchased at retail stores should be counted as local final demand. The ratio of local final demand to tourist spending is called the capture rate.

Capture rate = local final demand / tourism spending in local area

Capture rates, like multipliers, will vary with the size and nature of the region as well as the kind of tourist spending included. One must therefore be cautious in taking a multiplier or capture rate cited in one study and using it in another.

Another way of calculating a multiplier (generally the preferred approach among economists) is as a ratio of income or employment to sales. This kind of multiplier is sometimes called a Keynesian multiplier or response coefficient.

Type III Income multiplier =

$$\frac{\text{Total direct, indirect, and induced income}}{\text{direct sales}}$$

Type III Employment multiplier =

$$\frac{\text{Total direct, indirect, and induced employment}}{\text{direct sales}}$$

This income (employment) multiplier produces total income (employment) impacts when multiplied by the direct sales. One must still be careful in distinguishing between tourism spending/sales and direct sales effects. Some studies may embed the capture rate in the multiplier, expressing the ratio in terms of tourism spending rather than direct sales.

Measures of Economic Impacts

The economic impacts of tourism are typically estimated by some variation of the following simple formula:

Economic Impact of Tourism = Number of Tourists * Average Spending per Visitor * Multiplier

The formula suggests three distinct steps and corresponding measurements or models:

(1) *Estimate the change in the number and types of tourists to the region due to the proposed policy or action.* Estimates or projections of tourist activity generally come from a demand model or some system for measuring levels of tourism activity in an area. Economic impact estimates will rest heavily on good estimates of the numbers and types of visitors. These must come from carefully designed measurements of tourist activity, a good demand model, or good judgement. This step is usually the weakest link in most tourism impact studies, as few regions have accurate counts of tourists, let alone good models for predicting changes in

tourism activity or separating local visitors from visitors from outside the region.

(2) *Estimate average levels of spending (often within specific market segments) of tourists in the local area.* Spending averages come from sample surveys or are sometimes borrowed or adapted from other studies. Spending estimates must be based on a representative sample of the population of tourists taking into account variations across seasons, types of tourists, and locations within the study area. As spending can vary widely across different kinds of tourists, we recommend estimating average spending for a set of key tourist segments based on samples of at least 50-100 visitors within each tourism segment. Segments should be defined to capture differences in spending between local residents vs. tourists, day users vs. overnight visitors, type of accommodation (motel, campground, seasonal home, with friends and relatives), and type of transportation (car, RV, air, rail, etc.). In broadly based tourism impact studies, it is useful to identify unique spending patterns of important activity segments such as downhill skiers, boaters, convention & business travelers. Multiplying the number of tourists by the average spending per visitor (be careful the units are consistent) gives an estimate of total tourist spending in the area. Estimates of tourist spending will generally be more accurate if distinct spending profiles and use estimates are made for key tourism segments. The use and spending estimates are the two most important parts of an economic impact assessment. When combined, they capture the amount of money brought into the region by tourists. Multipliers are needed only if one is interested in the secondary effects of tourism spending.

(3) *Apply the change in spending to a regional economic model or set of multipliers to determine secondary effects.*

Secondary effects of tourism are estimated using multipliers or a model of the region's economy. Multipliers generally come from an economic base or input-output model of the region's economy. In many cases multipliers are borrowed (often improperly) or adjusted from published multipliers or other studies. One should not take a multiplier estimated for one region and apply it in a region with a quite different economic structure. Generally, multipliers are higher for larger regions with more diversified economies and lower for smaller regions with more limited economic development. A common error is to apply a statewide multiplier (since these are more widely published) to a local region. This will yield inflated estimates of local multiplier effects. Multipliers can also be used to convert estimates of spending or sales to income and employment. Simple ratios can be used to capture how much income or jobs are generated per dollar of sales. These ratios will vary from region to region and across individual economic sectors due to the relative importance of labor inputs in each industry and different wage and salary rates in different regions of the country. Be aware that job estimates are generally not full time equivalents, making them difficult to compare across industries with different proportions of seasonal and part time jobs. Income or value added are generally the preferred measures of the contribution of tourism to a region's economy.

4

Tourism and Biodiversity

Tourism is an important part of the global economy. According to the World Travel and Tourism Council, global travel and tourism directly and indirectly generates 11% of global GDP. This supports 200 million jobs, which accounts for 8% of the world's employment; an estimated 5.5 million new jobs will be created in tourism each year until 2010. The opportunities for tourism development continue to expand as the number of tourists increases, but tourism activities are not evenly distributed between or within different continents. However, tourism is a double-edged activity. It has the potential to contribute in a positive manner to socio-economic achievements but, at the same time, its fast and sometimes uncontrolled growth can be the major cause of degradation of the environment and loss of local identity and traditional cultures.

Biological and physical resources are in fact the assets that attract tourists. However, the stress imposed by tourism activities on fragile ecosystems accelerates and aggravates their depletion. Paradoxically, the very success of tourism may lead to the degradation of the natural environment: by depleting natural resources tourism reduces the site attractiveness to tourists, the very commodity that tourism has to offer.

Tropical countries need to use tourism benefits to encourage local people to support biodiversity conservation and sustainable management. This is one of the greatest challenges for development, which can be done especially where there are:

— relatively secure access or tenure rights over land and other biological resources (including exclusion rights) - this is fundamental to the local people's ability to participate in decisionmaking and gain benefits from tourism;

— local communities with the management and marketing skills to participate in tourism;

— direct linkages to the economy through employment of local labour, or purchase of local goods and services.

The nature of the link between local communities and economic development can alter the pattern of incentives to improve biodiversity use. Where local people earn significant income through participation in tourism, tourism can shift livelihood strategies away from unsustainable use of biological resources. But where benefits from tourism are smaller, they may be invested in activities that do not support biodiversity or even threaten it.

Serious disagreements over biological resource use may emerge, where some local groups benefit more than others. Tourism can reduce local access to natural resources, for example, where game-viewing leads to tighter access restrictions on the areas in which local people can harvest wild resources. This could have negative impacts on biodiversity by concentrating local resource use in smaller areas and/ or by undermining local management systems. The scope for improving livelihoods through tourism is therefore very variable, as are its impacts. In the wider development framework, tourism can be an important mechanism for stimulating private sector support for biodiversity conservation. It can also provide essential economic justification for improved biodiversity management, within and outside protected areas. Moreover, tourism can be a tool for enhancing public education and raising awareness of the value of local resources, especially where nationals are encouraged to participate in nature-based tourism.

As far as economic benefits are concerned, tourism certainly constitutes an opportunity for economic development, economic diversification and the growth of related activities, in developing countries especially, contributing around 1.5 per cent of world gross national product. Tourism is also a major source of income and employment. Tourism based on the natural environment is a vital growing segment of the tourism industry and, despite the negative impacts, and given the fact that tourism generates a large proportion of income and that a growing percentage of the activities are nature-based, tourism does present a significant potential for realizing benefits in terms of the conservation of biological diversity and the sustainable use of its components.

Among the benefits are direct revenues generated by fees and taxes incurred and voluntary payments for the use of biological resources. These revenues can be used for the maintenance of natural areas and the contribution of tourism to economic development, including linkage effects to other related sectors and job-creation. Sustainable tourism can make positive improvements to biological diversity conservation especially when local communities are directly involved with operators. If such local communities receive income directly from a tourist enterprise they, in turn, increase their evaluation of the resources around them. This is followed by greater protection and conservation of those resources as they are recognized as the source of income.

Moreover, sustainable tourism can serve as a major educational opportunity, increasing knowledge of and respect for natural ecosystems and biological resources. Other benefits include the provision of incentives for maintaining traditional arts and crafts, traditional knowledge, and innovations and practices that contribute to the sustainable use of biological diversity.

In considering the role of tourism in the sustainable use of biological resources and their diversity, it is important that the potential adverse impacts of tourism are fully considered. These are roughly divided into environmental impacts and socioeconomic impacts, the latter generally being those imposed on local and indigenous communities. Although such impacts on biological resources may be less easy to quantify and analyze systematically, they may be at least as important as, if not more important than, environmental impacts in the long term.

Direct use of natural resources, both renewable and non-renewable, in the provision of tourist facilities is one of the most significant direct impacts of tourism in a given area. Land use for accommodation and infrastructure provision, the choice of the site, the use of building materials are all essential factors. Deforestation and intensified or unsustainable use of land also cause erosion and loss of biodiversity.

Direct impact on the species composition and on wildlife can be caused by incorrect behaviors and unregulated tourism activities (e.g. off-road driving, plant-picking, hunting, shooting, fishing, scuba diving). Moreover, tourists and tourist transportation means can increase the risk of introducing alien species and the manner and frequency of human presence can cause disturbance to the behavior of animals. Construction activities related to tourism can cause enormous alteration to wildlife habitats and ecosystems.

Tourism has for many years been focused on mountain and coastal areas. Pressures from tourism activities on biological resources and their diversity are enormous and includes: erosion and pollution from the construction of hiking trails, bridges in high mountains, camp sites, chalet and hotels. Tourism activities have a major impact also on the marine and coastal environment, the resources they host and the diversity of those resources. Most often, those impacts are due to inappropriate planning, irresponsible behavior by tourists and operators and/or lack of education and awareness of the impacts by, for example, tourist resorts along the coastal zones.

Tourism is also a water-intensive activity with a large production of waste. The extraction of groundwater by some tourism activities can cause desiccation, resulting in loss of biological diversity. Moreover, the disposal of untreated effluents into surrounding rivers and seas can cause eutrophication and it can also introduce a large amount of pathogens into the water body. Disposal of waste produced by the tourism industry may cause major environmental problems.

Socioeconomic and cultural impacts of tourism include influx of people and related social degradation, impacts on local communities and on cultural values. Increased tourism activities can cause an influx of people seeking employment or entrepreneurial opportunities, but who may not be able to find suitable employment, thus causing social degradation.

Sudden loss of income and jobs can also be experienced in times of downturn, if the economy is not diversified and it heavily relies on tourism. When tourism development occurs, economic benefits are usually unequally distributed among members of local communities. In the case of foreign direct investment, much of the profit may be transferred back to the home country. Therefore, tourism can actually increase inequalities in communities, and thus relative poverty.

Tourism has a highly complex impact on cultural values. Tourism activities may lead to intergenerational conflicts and may affect gender relationships. Traditional practices and events may also be influenced by the tourist preferences. Tourism development can lead to the loss of access by indigenous and local communities to their land and resources as well as sacred sites.

Sustainable tourism is therefore in everybody's interest. Given that a high percentage of tourism involves visits to naturally and culturally distinguished sites, generating large amounts of revenue, there are clearly major opportunities for investing in the maintenance and sustainable use of biological resources. Along with the efforts to maximize benefits, efforts must be made to minimize the adverse impacts of the tourism industry on biological diversity.

Convention on Biological Diversity (CBD) Guidelines on Biodiversity and Tourism development

International guidelines for activities related to sustainable tourism development in vulnerable terrestrial, marine and coastal ecosystems and habitats of major importance for biological diversity and protected areas, including fragile riparian and mountain ecosystems

A. Scope

International guidelines for activities related to sustainable tourism development in vulnerable terrestrial, marine and coastal ecosystems and habitats of major importance for biological diversity and protected areas, including fragile riparian and mountain ecosystems

1. The present Guidelines are voluntary and represent a range of opportunities for local, regional, national governments, indigenous and local communities and other stakeholders to manage tourism activities in an ecological, economic and socially sustainable manner. They can be flexibly applied to suit different circumstances and domestic institutional and legal settings.
2. The Guidelines will assist Parties to the Convention on Biological Diversity, public authorities and stakeholders at all levels, to apply the provisions of the Convention to the sustainable development and management of tourism policies, strategies, projects and activities. They will provide technical guidance to policy makers, decision makers and managers with responsibilities covering tourism and/or biodiversity, whether in national or local government, the private sector, indigenous and local communities,(1) non-governmental organizations or other organizations, on a process for working together with key stakeholders involved in tourism and biodiversity.
3. The Guidelines cover all forms and activities of tourism. These activities should be consistent with the principles of conservation and sustainable use of biological diversity. These include, but are not limited to, conventional mass tourism, ecotourism, nature- and culture-based tourism, heritage and traditional tourism, cruise tourism, leisure and sports tourism. Although the primary focus of the Guidelines is vulnerable ecosystems and habitats, they are also appropriate for tourism with impact on biodiversity in all geographical locations and tourist destinations. The guidelines on Biodiversity and Tourism Development can also play a crucial role in incorporating sustainable use and equity strategies within and around protected areas. Furthermore the Guidelines recognize the need

for collaboration between originating and receiving countries and should be used to balance local interests and national, regional and international policies..

B. The Policy-making, Development Planning and Management Process

4. The main elements considered in developing the Guidelines are:
   a. Framework for management of tourism and biodiversity;
   b. Notification process in relation to such a management framework;
   c. Public education, capacity-building and awareness-raising concerning tourism and biodiversity.

5. Policy-making, development planning and the management process need to be undertaken through a multi-stakeholder process. Governments will normally coordinate this process at national level. This process may also be undertaken at more local levels by local government, and should ensure strong involvement of indigenous and local communities throughout the management and decision-making process. In addition, those responsible for tourism development and activities are encouraged to consult with and involve all relevant stakeholders, and especially those who are or may be affected by such developments and activities. The process applies to both new tourism development and the management of the existing tourism operations. Institutions

6. In order to ensure coordination between the levels of decision-making in government departments and agencies concerned with management of biological diversity and tourism as well as agencies responsible

for broader national economic development, inter- and intra-departmental and inter-organizational structures and processes should be established, if they do not already exist, to guide policy development and implementation.

7. There is a need to improve awareness and exchange of knowledge between those responsible for and affected by tourism and nature conservation at a national, subnational and local level. In addition, national biodiversity strategies and action plans should include consideration of tourism issues, and tourism plans should likewise include full consideration of biodiversity issues. Existing documents, strategies and plans should be coherent or revised and amended to that effect as applicable.

8. A consultative process should be established to ensure ongoing and effective dialogue and information-sharing with stakeholders, as well as to resolve conflicts that might arise in relation to tourism and biological diversity and build consensus. To assist in this process, a multi-stakeholder body should be established including government departments, the tourism sector, non-governmental organizations, indigenous and local communities and other stakeholders, to ensure their engagement and full participation in the whole process, and encourage the establishment of partnerships.

9. The institutional arrangements should provide for the comprehensive involvement of stakeholders in the management process described in these Guidelines.

10. Authorities and managers of protected areas have a special role for the management of tourism and biodiversity. To this end, there is a need for government support and resources for managers,

including training to perform their role effectively. In addition, it is necessary to establish and review mechanisms and funding policies to ensure the availability of adequate resources for maintaining biodiversity and promoting sustainable tourism. International institutions and development agencies should be involved as appropriate.

11. To be sustainable, tourism development in any destination requires coordinated policy-making, development planning and management. The policy-making, development planning and management process comprises the following steps:

    a. Baseline information and review;
    b. Vision and goals;
    c. Objectives;
    d. Review of legislation and control measures;
    e. Impact assessment;
    f. Impact management and mitigation;
    g. Decision-making;
    h. Implementation;
    i. Monitoring and reporting;
    j. Adaptive management.

1.Baseline information

12. Baseline information is necessary to enable informed decisions to be taken on any issue. A minimum of baseline information is needed to enable impact assessment and decision-making and it is recommended that its compilation follow the ecosystem approach.

13. For tourism and biodiversity, the baseline information should include information, as appropriate, on:

    a. Current economic, social and environmental conditions at national and local level, including current and planned tourism development and activities and their overall positive and negative impacts, as well as development and activities in other sectors;

    b. Structure and trends within the tourism sector, tourism policy and tourism markets and trends, at national, regional and international level, including information based on market research as necessary;

    c. Environmental and biodiversity resources and processes, including any special features and sites of particular importance and protected areas, and identifying those resources that may be off bounds to development due to their particular fragility and those resources identified by existing analysis of threats;

    d. Culturally sensitive areas;

    e. Benefits from, and costs of, tourism to indigenous and local communities;

    f. Information on damage done to the environment in the past;

    g. National biodiversity strategies, action plans and reports and other sectoral plans and policies relevant for tourism development and biodiversity;

    h. National, subnational and local sustainable-development plans.

14. Baseline information should take into consideration all sources of knowledge. The adequacy of the baseline

information available will need to be reviewed, and where necessary, further research and information-gathering can be undertaken to fill gaps that may be identified.

15. All stakeholders may contribute relevant information to this process, including indigenous and local communities. To this end, there is a need for capacity-building and training to assist stakeholders in documenting, accessing, analysing and interpreting baseline information.

16. Collation and synthesis of information provided will need to be undertaken by an appropriately qualified team, drawing on a range of expertise, including expertise in tourism and in biodiversity issues, and in traditional knowledge and innovation systems.

17. In order to ensure that all relevant information, its credibility and reliability, are considered, all stakeholders should be involved in review of the collated baseline information available, and in the synthesis of this information.

18. Baseline information should include maps, geographical information systems and other visual tools, including already identified zoning schemes.

19. The baseline information-gathering and review process should make full use of the clearing-house mechanism under the Convention on Biological Diversity, as well as other relevant networks such as the World Network of Biosphere Reserves, World Heritage sites and Ramsar sites.

20. Requirements for site-specific information in relation to proposals for tourism development and activities at particular locations are set out in the notification process, and its compilation should follow the ecosystem approach. To enable impact assessment and

decision making, the basic information required includes:

a. Site-specific aspects:

i. The various laws and regulations and plans that may be applicable to the specific site, including overviews of:

   a. Existing laws at local, subnational and national levels;

   b. Existing uses, customs and traditions;

   c. Relevant regional and international conventions or agreements and their status, and cross-boundary agreements or memoranda of understanding (MoUs);

ii. Identification of various stakeholders involved in or potentially affected by the proposed project - including stakeholders in governmental, non-governmental, and private sectors (particularly those from the tourism sector), and indigenous and local communities - along with details concerning their participation in and/or consultation on the proposed project during its design, planning, construction and operation;

b. Ecological aspects:

i. Detailed indication of the protected and biodiversity significant areas;

ii. Specifications on the ecosystems, habitats, species;

iii. Quantitative and qualitative information on the loss of habitats and species (main reasons, trends);

iv. Indexing of species;

v. Identified threats;

vi. Existing zones, ecological zones and existing tourism zones within the ecological zones;

vii. Ecologically sensitive zones and zones where ecological disasters have or will most likely take place;

c. *Development aspects:*

i. Summary of the proposed project, why and by whom it is proposed, estimated outcomes and possible impacts (including impacts on the surrounding areas and transboundary impacts), and quantitative and qualitative data on these aspects;

ii. Description of the stages of development and the various structures and stakeholders that may be involved at each stage;

iii. Description of current land-uses, infrastructures, tourism facilities and services and their interaction with proposed operations.

2. *Vision and goals*

Vision:

An overall vision for sustainable tourism development in harmony with the goals and objectives of the Convention on Biological Diversity and other related conventions, such as the World Heritage Convention, is important for the effective management of tourism and biodiversity, and for ensuring that this also contributes to income generation and poverty reduction and a reduction of threats to biodiversity. The vision developed at the local level, while reflecting local priorities and realities, should take into account, as appropriate, national and regional tourism development strategies, policies and plans for economic and social development and for land-use, as well as the baseline information and review. It should be based on a multi-stakeholder process including indigenous and local communities that are or may be affected by tourism development.

Goals:

The main goals are established to maximize the positive benefits of tourism to biodiversity, ecosystems, and economic and social development, and of biodiversity to tourism, while minimizing negative social and environmental impacts from tourism, and can cover, inter alia:

a) Maintenance of the structure and functioning of ecosystems;

b) Sustainable tourism compatible with biodiversity conservation and sustainable use;

c) Fair and equitable sharing of benefits of tourism activities, with emphasis on the specific needs of the indigenous and local communities concerned;

d) Integration and interrelation with other plans, developments or activities in the same area;

e) Information and capacity-building;

f) Poverty reduction, through the generation of sufficient revenues and employment to effectively reduce threats to biodiversity in indigenous and local communities;

g) Protection of indigenous livelihoods, resources and of access to those resources;

h) Diversification of economic activities beyond tourism to reduce dependency on tourism;

i) Prevention of any lasting damage to biological diversity, ecosystems, and natural resources, and of social and cultural damage, and restoration of past damage where appropriate;

j) Supporting the effective participation and involvement of representatives of indigenous and local communities in the development, operation and monitoring of tourism activities on lands and waters traditionally occupied by them

k) Zoning and control of tourism developments and activities, including licensing and overall targets for and limits to the scale of tourism, to provide a range of activities for user groups that meet overall visions and goals;

l) Empowerment through participation in decision-making;

m) Access by indigenous and local communities to infrastructure, transport, communications and healthcare provisions laid on for tourists;

n) Increased safety for indigenous local communities;

o) Increased social pride;

p) Control of tourism development and activities including licensing and clear indication on the limits to the scale and type of tourism development.

23. In relation to sharing of benefits arising from tourism and the conservation of biodiversity with indigenous and local communities, it should be noted that benefits may take various forms, including: job creation, fostering local enterprises, participation in tourism enterprises and projects, education, direct investment opportunities, economic linkages and ecological services. Appropriate mechanisms need to be established/ evolved to capture the benefits.

24. The vision and goals will form the basis of national strategies or master plans for sustainable development of tourism in relation to biodiversity. Such plans should also incorporate consideration of biodiversity

strategies and plans. In addition, biodiversity strategies and plans should include consideration of tourism issues.

25. Governments will normally coordinate this process at national level. This process may also be undertaken at more local levels by local government, and by communities at community level. Where local and community level vision and goals for tourism and biodiversity have been set, these may be taken into account by governments when preparing the national level vision and goals, for example through workshops at the local level.

3. Objectives

26. The objectives focus on actions to implement specific elements of the overall vision and goals, and may include clear activities and the time by which these will be achieved. Objectives should be performance-based (e.g., construction of an interpretative trail to aid development of local guide services) and process-based (e.g., establishment of an operational management system for tourism and biodiversity). As with the vision and goals, it is important to involve and consult with all relevant stakeholders, and especially the tourism industry and indigenous and local communities that are or may be affected by tourism development, in the process for setting objectives.

27. Objectives should be specific and should include specific areas identified in clearly delineated zones listing the types of activities and infrastructure that would be acceptable and should be developed. It should also outline the impact management measures that would be appropriate, and intended markets (with greater detail, as set out in the notification process,

being required for proposals for tourism development or activities at specific locations).

28. Governments may also wish to consider:

a. Measures to ensure that sites designated at international level, such as Ramsar or World Heritage sites or Biosphere Reserves, are accorded appropriate legal recognition and government assistance at the national level;

b. Establishing reserves based on the biosphere reserve concept and incorporating sustainable-development objectives, generating income and employment opportunities for indigenous and local communities, and promoting appropriate product development;

c. Measures to ensure that sites, at the national level, such as national parks, reserves and marine conservation areas are accorded appropriate legal recognition, have management plans and are provided necessary government support;

d. Strengthening the protected area network and encouraging the role of protected areas as key locations for good practices in the management of sustainable tourism and biodiversity, taking into account the full range of protected area categories;

e. Use of political and economic tools and measures to encourage the channelling of part of total tourism revenues towards supporting the conservation and sustainable use of biodiversity, such as conservation of protected areas, education, research programmes, or local community development;

f. Encouraging all stakeholders, as well as the private sector, to actively support the conservation of biodiversity and the sustainable use of its components.

29. Governments will normally coordinate this process at national level. This process may also be undertaken at more local levels by local government, and by communities at community level. Where local- and community-level objectives for tourism and biodiversity have been set, these may be taken into account by governments when preparing national level objectives.

4. Legislation and control measures

30. Respect for existing national legislation and appropriate regulatory mechanisms and tools, such as land-use planning, protected area management plans, environmental assessment, building regulations and standards for sustainable tourism, are essential for the effective implementation of any overall vision, goals, and objectives. A review of legislation and control measures could consider, as appropriate, the legislation and control measures available for implementation of the overall vision, goals and objectives for tourism and biodiversity, their effectiveness, including enforcement, and any gaps that may need to be addressed for example, by revision of-or the development of additional-legislation and control measures.

31. The review of legislation and control measures may include, inter alia, assessment of the effectiveness of any provisions for resource management, access, and/ or ownership by communities, especially indigenous and local communities in relation to tourism development or operations on lands and waters traditionally occupied or used by them;; addressing legally established rights of indigenous and local communities; and enabling these groups to make decisions about tourism development and activities, amongst other forms of development and activities, in these areas.

32. Legislation and control measures considered could include measures for:

   a. Effective enforcement of existing laws, including the participation of all stakeholders;

   b. Approval and licensing processes for tourism development and activities;

   c. Controlling the planning, siting, design and construction of tourism facilities and infrastructures;

   d. Management of tourism in relation to biodiversity and ecosystems, including vulnerable areas;

   e. Application of environmental assessment, including assessment of cumulative impacts and effects on biodiversity, to all proposed tourism developments, and as a tool to develop policies and measure their impacts;

   f. Setting national standards and/or criteria for tourism that are consistent with overall national or regional plans for sustainable development and national biodiversity strategies and action plans:

      i. Environmental quality and land-use criteria in and around tourism sites;

      ii. Development of a decision-making process with environmental and cultural sustainability guidelines for new and existing tourism development within the designated goals and objectives of the site's different zones and within the limits of acceptable change;

   g. Integrated land-use management;

   h. Ensuring inter-linkages between tourism and cross-cutting issues, including agricultural development, coastal zone management, water resources, etc.;

i. Mechanisms to resolve any inconsistencies between policy objectives and/or legislation in a manner that takes into account the interests of all stakeholders;

j. Application of economic instruments, including tiered user fees, bonds, taxes or levies, for the management of tourism and biodiversity;

k. Creating incentives for sustainable tourism development in line with the provisions of the Convention on Biological Diversity and Agenda 21 through relevant economic mechanisms;

l. Supporting private sector voluntary initiatives consistent with these Guidelines, such as certification schemes and providing opportunities for the private tourism sector to contribute to management initiatives through direct donations, in-kind services, and other voluntary initiatives consistent with these Guidelines, and relevant policies;

m. Avoiding tourism development or activities outside those areas set out in the objectives;

n. Monitoring, control of and provision of information on activities related to collection and trade of biological and related cultural resources within tourism sites.

33. Governments will normally coordinate this process at the national level. It is important to involve and consult with all relevant stakeholders, and especially indigenous and local communities that are or may be affected by tourism development, in the process for reviewing legislation and control measures, assessing their adequacy and effectiveness, and proposing development of new legislation and measures where necessary.

5. Impact assessment

34. Impact assessment for sustainable tourism development in ecosystems should be based on the "Guidelines for incorporating biodiversity-related issues into environmental impact assessment legislation and/or processes and in strategic environmental assessment" developed by the Convention on Biological Diversity and contained in the annex to decision VI/7 A (paras. 1 24) as well as on the Akwe: Kon voluntary guidelines for the conduct of cultural, environmental and social impact assessment regarding developments proposed to take place on, or which are likely to impact on, sacred sites and on lands and waters traditionally occupied or used by indigenous and local communities (as contained in Annex to Decision VII/14).

35. At national level, Governments should normally undertake assessment of impacts associated with the overall vision, goals and objectives for tourism and biodiversity. In addition, this process may also be undertaken at more local levels by local government, and by indigenous and local communities.

36. Proposers of tourism developments or activities should assess the potential impacts of their proposals and provide information on this through a notification process.

37. Governments will normally undertake evaluations of the adequacy of impact assessments submitted by proposers of tourism developments or activities. These evaluations will need to be undertaken by an appropriately qualified team, drawing on a range of expertise, including expertise in tourism and in biodiversity management, and also involving those indigenous and local communities that would be

affected by the proposals. There should be public access to the documentation.

38. If the information provided is not sufficient, or the impact assessment inadequate, then further impact assessment studies may need to be undertaken. The proposer may be requested to undertake such studies, or the Government may decide to undertake these studies, and may request funds from the proposer for this purpose, as appropriate. Other stakeholders, including biodiversity managers and indigenous and local communities that may be affected by a proposed development, may also provide their assessments of impacts associated with specific proposals for tourism developments or activities, and provisions may be needed to ensure that any such assessments are taken into account by decision-makers.

39. Indigenous and local communities concerned should be involved in impact assessment. Their traditional knowledge should be acknowledged and considered for impact assessment in particular tourism projects that affect their sacred sites or lands and waters traditionally occupied or used by them.

40. Sufficient time should be allowed considering the different conditions and circumstances to ensure that all stakeholders are able to participate effectively in the decision-making process for any project using information provided by the impact assessment. Such information should be provided in forms that are accessible and comprehensible to all the various stakeholders involved.

41. Impacts of tourism in relation to the environment and biological diversity may include:

   a. Use of land and resources for accommodation, tourism facilities and other infrastructure provision, including road networks, airports and seaports;

b. Extraction and use of building materials (e.g., use of sand from beaches, reef limestone and wood);

c. Damage to or destruction of ecosystems and habitats, including deforestation, draining of wetlands, and intensified or unsustainable use of land;

d. Increased risk of erosion;

e. Disturbance of wild species, disrupting normal behaviour and potentially affecting mortality and reproductive success;

f. Alterations to habitats and ecosystems;

g. Increased risk of fires;

h. Unsustainable consumption of flora and fauna by tourists (e.g., through picking of plants; or purchase of souvenirs manufactured from wildlife, in particular such endangered species as corals and turtle shells; or through unregulated hunting, shooting and fishing);

i. Increased risk of introduction of alien species;

j. Intensive water demand from tourism;

k. Extraction of groundwater;

l. Deterioration in water quality (freshwater, coastal waters) and sewage pollution;

m. Eutrophication of aquatic habitats;

n. Introduction of pathogens;

o. Generation, handling and disposal of sewage and waste-water;

p. Chemical wastes, toxic substances and pollutants;

q. Solid waste (garbage or rubbish);

r. Contamination of land, freshwater and seawater resources;

s. Pollution and production of greenhouse gases, resulting from travel by air, road, rail, or sea, at local, national and global levels;

t. Noise.

42. Socio-economic and cultural impacts related to tourism may include:

a. Influx of people and social degradation (e.g. local prostitution, drug abuse, etc.);

b. Impacts on children and youth;

c. Vulnerability to the changes in the flow of tourist arrivals which may result in sudden loss of income and jobs in times of downturn;

d. Impacts on indigenous and local communities and cultural values;

e. Impacts on health and the integrity of local cultural systems;

f. Intergenerational conflicts and changed gender relationships;

g. Erosion of traditional practices and lifestyles;

h. Loss of access by indigenous and local communities to their land and resources as well as sacred sites, which are integral to the maintenance of traditional knowledge systems and traditional lifestyles.

43. The potential benefits of tourism may include:

a. Revenue creation for the maintenance of natural resources of the area;

b. Contributions to economic and social development, for example:

i. Funding the development of infrastructure and services;

ii. Providing jobs;

iii. Providing funds for development or maintenance of sustainable practices;

iv. Providing alternative and supplementary ways for communities to receive revenue from biological diversity;

v. Generating incomes;

vi. Education and empowerment;

vii. An entry product that can have direct benefits for developing other related products at the site and regionally;

viii. Tourist satisfaction and experience gained at tourist destination.

6. Impact management and mitigation

44. Impact management is essential to avoid or minimize any potential damage to biodiversity conservation and sustainable use that tourism development or activities might cause. Proposals for tourism development or activities may incorporate proposals for impact management, but these may not necessarily be judged sufficient to deal with potential impacts on biodiversity. Therefore all stakeholders, and especially Governments that exercise overall control over tourism development and activities, will need to consider the various impact management approaches that may be necessary in any given situation. In particular, Governments should be aware that the tourism industry could provide a direct impetus for conservation of vulnerable ecosystems by supporting

sustainable tourism activities that have a direct commercial interest in maintaining the vulnerable ecosystem in a good condition.

45. Tourism should be planned and managed using the internationally accepted planning methodologies (such as the Recreation Opportunity Spectrum and the Limits of Acceptable Change). In vulnerable ecosystems, based on these methodologies and relevant background information, tourism should be restricted and where necessary prevented.

46. Impact management can include, inter alia, measures for the siting of tourism development and activities, including establishing appropriate activities in different designated zones, differentiation between the impacts of different types of tourism, and measures to control tourist flows in and around tourist destinations and key sites, to promote appropriate behaviour by tourists so as to minimize their impacts, and to establish limits to numbers of visitors and their impacts within Limits of Acceptable Change at any site.

47. Impact management in relation to transboundary ecosystems and migratory species requires regional cooperation.

48. There is a need to identify those who will be responsible for implementing impact management and the resources that will be required for impact management.

49. Impact management for tourism development and activities can include the adoption and effective implementation of policies, good practices and lessons learned that cover, inter alia:

   a. Controlling impacts of major tourist flows including excursions, cruise ships, etc., which can cause serious effects on destinations even though they are visited for only short periods;

b. Reducing impacts of activities outside tourism areas on adjacent and other ecosystems of importance for tourism (e.g., pollution from nearby farming activities or extractive industries may affect areas of tourism development);

c. Responsible use of natural resources (e.g., land, soil, energy, water);

d. Reducing, minimizing and preventing pollution and waste (e.g. solid and liquid waste, emissions to air, transport);

e. Promoting the design of facilities that are more eco-efficient, which adopt the cleaner production approach, and use environmentally sound technologies, in particular to reduce emissions of carbon dioxide and other greenhouse gases and ozone-depleting substances, as set out in international agreements;

f. Conserving flora, fauna and ecosystems;

g. Preventing the introduction of alien species as a result of the construction, landscaping and operating of tourism activities, including for example from shipping associated with tourism;

h. Conserving landscapes, cultural and natural heritage;

i. Respecting the integrity of local cultures and avoiding negative effects on social structures, involving, and cooperating with, indigenous and local communities, including measures to ensure respect for sacred sites and customary users of these sites, and to prevent negative impacts on them and on lands and waters traditionally occupied or used by them, as well as on their subsistence resources;

j. Using local products and skills, and providing local employment;

k. Promoting appropriate behaviour by tourists so as to minimize their adverse impacts, and to promote positive effects through education, interpretation, extension, and other means of awareness raising;

l. Alignment of marketing strategies and messages with the principles of sustainable tourism;

m. Contingency plans for handling accidents, emergencies or bankruptcies that may occur during construction and use of facilities and which may threaten the environment and the conservation and sustainable use of biodiversity;

n. Environmental and cultural sustainability audits and review of existing tourism activities and developments and of the effectiveness with which impact management is being applied to existing tourism activities and developments;

o. Mitigation measures for existing impacts, and appropriate funding to support them. Such measures should include development and implementation of compensation measures in cases when tourism has resulted in negative environmental, cultural, and socio-economic effects, taking into consideration the range of redress and compensation measures.

50. Governments, in cooperation with biodiversity managers, those communities that would be affected by the proposals, and other stakeholders, would normally assess the need for impact management in addition to any management measures included in the

proposals under consideration. All stakeholders should understand the importance of such impact management.

51. The tourism industry can assist in promoting corporate policies on sustainable tourism and biodiversity, with defined goals, monitoring and reporting their progress publicly on a regular basis.

7. Decision-making

52. Decisions will be made concerning approval or otherwise of, inter alia:

    a. National strategies and plans for tourism and biodiversity;
    b. Proposals for tourism development and activities at particular locations in relation to biodiversity, which are to be submitted through the notification process;
    c. Adequacy of impact management measures in relation to anticipated impacts from tourism development and activities;
    d. Adequacy and frequency of monitoring and reporting.

53. Such decisions will ultimately be taken by Governments (or specific authorities designated by Governments). It is recognized, however, that effective consultation with and participation of the communities and groups affected, including specific input from biodiversity managers, and from indigenous and local communities as well as the private sector in a broad sense, is an important foundation of the decision-making process and critical to sustainable development. Decision makers should consider using

multi-stakeholder processes as a tool for the decision-making process.

54. The decision-making process should be transparent, accountable, and apply the precautionary approach. Legal mechanisms should be put in place for notification and approval of tourism development proposals and for ensuring implementation of the conditions of approval of development proposals.

55. For proposals for tourism development and activities at particular locations, the proposers will normally be required to provide the information set out in the notification process. This should apply equally to public-sector development and infrastructure projects, as well as to private-sector development. Impact assessment should be a component of any decision-making process.

56. Measures should be taken to ensure full and timely disclosure of project information concerning tourism development proposals. Consistent with Article 8(j), decision-making should include meaningful consultation with indigenous and local communities affected by projects in order to ensure, inter alia, respect for the customs and traditional knowledge, innovations and practices of indigenous and local communities, and adequate funding and technical support for effective participation. Where the national legal regime requires prior informed consent of indigenous and local communities with respect to decisions identified in paragraph 52, such prior informed consent must be obtained.

57. Decisions should include a review of the adequacy of information available, that could cover, inter alia, baseline information, impact assessment, and information on the proposed tourism development or activity, its nature and size, the type(s) of tourism

involved, and information on human settlements and communities that may be affected.

58. In cases where there is not sufficient contextual/ baseline information available at the time, or where the overall vision, goals and objectives for tourism and biodiversity have not been developed sufficiently to make a decision, decisions may be deferred pending sufficient information being obtained, and/or completion of overall plans/goals.

59. In making a decision, conditions may be attached to any approvals that may be granted, including conditions regarding management of tourism in relation to avoidance or minimization of adverse impacts on biodiversity, and for appropriate decommissioning of tourism activities should the development cease. Decision makers may also, as appropriate, request further information from a proposer; defer a decision pending further baseline research by other agencies; or refuse a proposal.

8. Implementation

60. Implementation follows a decision to approve a particular proposal, strategy or plan. Unless otherwise stated, the developer and/or operator will be responsible for complying with the conditions for granting the approval; and, as part of this process, they can also be required to notify the designated government authority of any failures to comply with conditions attached to an approval, including conditions for decommissioning, and/or of any changes in circumstances, including unforeseen environmental conditions and/or biodiversity issues (e.g., detection of rare or endangered species not recorded in the original proposal and impact assessment).

61. Any revisions or changes to an approved project, including additions and/or variations of activities, must be approved by the designated authorities before construction.

62. Implementation plans should recognize that indigenous and local communities and other relevant stakeholders may require assistance as actors in implementation, and should ensure that sufficient resources are available for implementation and for effective participation.

63. Local stakeholders should be given an ongoing opportunity to express their wishes and concerns to those managing tourism facilities and activities. As part of this process, clear and adequate information regarding implementation should be provided for review by the stakeholders, in forms that are accessible and comprehensible to them.

64. Availability of information on policies, programmes, projects, and their implementation, including information on existing and future guidelines, should be ensured and exchange of information fostered, for example, through the clearing house mechanism of the Convention on Biological Diversity.

9. Monitoring and reporting

65. It is necessary to establish a monitoring and control system for the management of tourism activities and biological diversity. Long-term monitoring and assessment are necessary in relation to the impacts of tourism on biodiversity, and will need to take into account the timescale for ecosystem changes to become evident. Some effects may develop quickly, while others may take place more slowly. Long-term monitoring and assessment provide a means for

detecting adverse effects that may arise from tourism activities and development in relation to biodiversity, so that action can be taken to control and mitigate such effects.

66. Monitoring and surveillance in relation to management of tourism and biodiversity includes, inter alia, the following main areas:

   a. Implementation of approved tourism developments or activities, and compliance with any conditions attached when approval was granted, and taking appropriate actions in cases of non-compliance;

   b. Impacts of tourism activities on biodiversity and ecosystems, taking appropriate preventative actions as necessary;

   c. Impacts of tourism on the surrounding population, especially indigenous and local communities;

   d. General tourism activities and trends, including tour operations, tourism facilities, and tourist flows in originating and receiving countries, including progress towards sustainable tourism;

   e. Clearly defined objectives, actions and targets for conservation or mitigation of threats to biodiversity, maintenance or restoration of ecosystems and for tourism;

   f. Compliance with, and enforcement as necessary, of conditions attached to any approval. Communities and other interested stakeholders may also monitor and report their findings to the designated government authorities.

67. Developers and operators of tourism facilities and activities should be required to report periodically to designated authorities and to the public on compliance with conditions set out in approvals, and on the

condition of biodiversity and the environment in relation to the tourism facilities and activities for which they are responsible.

68. Prior to the commencement of any new tourism development or activities, an inclusive monitoring and reporting system should be put in place, with indicators to track how tourism actions are mitigating threats to biodiversity, along with agreed upon quantifiable standards indicating thresholds of acceptable change. These should be developed in conjunction with all key stakeholders including indigenous and local communities.

69. Indicators to cover aspects of management of biodiversity and sustainable tourism, including socio-economic and cultural aspects, should be identified and monitored at global, national, and local levels, and should include, but not be limited to, the following:

    a. Conservation of biodiversity;

    b. Generation of income and employment from tourism (long-term and short-term);

    c. Proportion of tourism income retained in the local community;

    d. Effectiveness of multi-stakeholder processes for management of biodiversity and sustainable tourism;

    e. Effectiveness of impact management;

    f. Contribution of tourism to the well-being of the local population;

    g. Visitor impacts and visitor satisfaction.

70. Monitoring results depend largely on the appropriate set of data to be collected. Guidelines on how to collect data in a way that can be used to evaluate change over

time should be developed. Monitoring could follow a standard process and format, and be based on a framework including parameters on social, economic, environmental and cultural impact.

71. Monitoring and surveillance in relation to biodiversity impacts should include activities undertaken to ensure respect for endangered species under relevant international agreements, prevention of the introduction of alien species as a result of tourism activities, compliance with national rules concerning access to genetic resources, and prevention of illegal and unauthorised removal of genetic resources.

72. In relation to indigenous and local communities, monitoring and evaluation should include development and use of appropriate tools to monitor and evaluate tourism impacts on the economy of indigenous and local communities, particularly their food and health security, traditional knowledge, practices and customary livelihoods. Use of indicators and early warning systems should be developed as appropriate, taking into account traditional knowledge, innovation and practices of indigenous and local communities, and guidelines developed under the Convention on Biological Diversity relating to traditional knowledge. Measures should also be taken to ensure that indigenous and local communities involved in, or affected by tourism, have the opportunity to be involved effectively in monitoring and evaluation.

73. Monitoring of general environmental and biodiversity conditions and trends, as well as tourism trends and impacts, can be undertaken by Governments, including designated biodiversity managers. Management measures may need to be adjusted, as appropriate, where adverse impacts on biodiversity and ecosystems

are detected. The need for and nature of such adjustments will be based on the results of monitoring, and it is important for these to be determined in dialogue with all relevant stakeholders, including the developers and/or operators of tourism facilities and activities, communities affected by those facilities and activities, and other interested stakeholders. The monitoring process needs to be multi-stakeholder and transparent.

10. Adaptive management

74. The ecosystem approach requires adaptive management to deal with the complex and dynamic nature of ecosystems and the absence of complete knowledge or understanding of their functioning. Ecosystem processes are often non-linear, and the outcome of such processes often shows time-lags. The result is discontinuities, leading to surprise and uncertainty. Management must be adaptive in order to be able to respond to such uncertainties and contain elements of "learning-by-doing" or research feedback. Measures may need to be taken even when some cause-and-effect relationships are not yet fully established scientifically.

75. Ecosystem processes and functions are complex and variable. Their level of uncertainty is increased by the interaction with social constructs, which need to be better understood. Therefore, ecosystem management must involve a learning process, which helps to adapt methodologies and practices to the ways in which these systems are being managed and monitored. Adaptive management should also take the precautionary approach fully into account.

76. Implementation programmes should be designed to adjust to the unexpected, rather than to act on the basis of a belief in certainties.

77. Ecosystem management needs to recognize the diversity of social and cultural factors affecting natural-resource use and sustainability.

78. Similarly, there is a need for flexibility in policy-making and implementation. Long-term, inflexible decisions are likely to be inadequate or even destructive. Ecosystem management should be envisaged as a long-term experiment that builds on its results as it progresses. This 'learning-by-doing" will also serve as an important source of information to gain knowledge of how best to monitor the results of management and evaluate whether established goals are being attained. In this respect, it would be desirable to establish or strengthen capacities of Parties for monitoring. In addition, adaptive management learning portfolios should be developed between different sites so that comparison can be made and lessons learned.

79. Implementing adaptive management in relation to tourism and biodiversity will require the active cooperation of all stakeholders in tourism, and especially those in the private sector, with biodiversity managers. Impacts on biodiversity at a particular location may require rapid curtailment of visits by tourists to prevent further damage, and to allow for recovery, and in the longer-term, may necessitate an overall reduction in tourist flows. It may be possible for tourists to be redirected to less sensitive areas in such cases. In all cases, maintenance of the balance between tourism and biodiversity will require close interaction between tourism managers and biodiversity managers, and appropriate frameworks for management and dialogue are likely to need to be established.

80. Governments, including designated biodiversity managers, in conjunction with all other stakeholders will therefore need to take actions, as appropriate, to address any problems encountered and to keep on track towards agreed goals. This may include changes and additions to conditions set in the original approval, and will require participation of and consultation with the developer and/or operator of the tourism facilities and activities concerned, and with local communities.
81. Adaptive management can also be undertaken by all those who have management control over any specific site, including local governments, indigenous and local communities, the private sector, non-governmental organizations and other organizations.
82. Where necessary, legal frameworks may need to be reviewed and amended to support adaptive management, taking into account experience gained.

C. Notification Process and Information Requirements

83. Proposals for tourism development and activities at particular locations in relation to biodiversity are to be submitted through the notification process. As such, this process provides the link between proposers of tourism activities and development, and the management process steps outlined above. In particular, the notification process makes specific links to the steps in the management process for impact assessment and decision-making and should take into account local, regional and national impacts. Proposers of tourism projects, including government agencies, should provide full and timely advance notice to all stakeholders who may be affected, including indigenous and local communities, of proposed developments.

84. Information to be provided as part of the notification could include:

a. Scale and types of tourism development or activities proposed, including a summary of the proposed project, why and by whom it is proposed, estimated outcomes and possible impacts, and a description of the stages of development and the various structures and stakeholders that may be involved at each stage;

b. Analysis of market for proposed tourism development or activities, based on market conditions and trends;

c. Geographical description including recreation opportunity zones, outlining tourist activities and infrastructure development, and location of the site of tourism development or activities, the identity and any special features of the surrounding environments and biodiversity;

d. Nature and extent of human-resource requirements and plans for their procurement;

e. Identification of various stakeholders involved in or potentially affected by the proposed project - including stakeholders in governmental, non-governmental, and private sectors, and indigenous and local communities - along with details concerning their participation in and/or consultation on the proposed project during its design, planning, construction and operation;

f. The perceived roles of local stakeholders in the proposed development;

g. The various laws and regulations that may be applicable to the specific site, including overviews of existing laws at local, subnational and national levels, of existing uses and customs, of relevant regional and international conventions or agreements and their status, and cross-boundary agreements or memoranda or understanding and any proposed legislation;

h. The proximity of the site to human settlements and communities, sites used by people from those settlements and communities as part of their livelihoods and traditional activities, and heritage, cultural or sacred sites;

i. Any flora, fauna and ecosystems that could be affected by the tourism development or activities, including keystone, rare, endangered or endemic species;

j. Ecological aspects of the site and its surroundings, including indication of any protected areas; specifications on the ecosystems, habitats, and species; quantitative and qualitative information on the loss of habitats and species (main reasons, trends), and indexing of species;

k. Training and supervision of personnel carrying out the tourism development or activities;

l. Likelihood of impacts beyond the immediate area of the tourism development or activities, including transboundary impacts and effects on migratory species;

m. A description of current environmental and socio-economic conditions;

n. Expected changes to environmental and socio-economic conditions as a result of the tourism development or activities;

o. Proposed management measures to avoid or minimize adverse impacts from the tourism development or activities, including verification of their functioning;

p. Proposed measures for mitigation, decommissioning and compensation in the event of problems arising with the tourism development or activities;

q. Proposed measures to maximize the local benefits of the tourism development or activities on surrounding human settlements and communities, biodiversity and ecosystems, which may include, but are not limited to:

   i. Using local products and skills;

   ii. Employment;

   iii. Restoration of biodiversity and ecosystems;

r. Relevant information from any previous tourism development or activities in the region, and information on possible cumulative effects;

s. Relevant information from any previous tourism development or activities by the proposer.

85. Categories of responses that Governments may wish to consider making in response to notification of proposals for, and requests for permission to undertake, tourism development, include, inter alia:

   a. Approval without conditions;

   b. Approval with conditions;

   c. Request for further information;

   d. Deferral pending further baseline research by other agencies;

   e. Refusal of the proposal.

D. Education, Capacity-building and Awareness-raising

86. Education and awareness-raising campaigns need to be addressed to both the professional sectors and the general public and should inform them about the impacts of tourism on biological diversity, and good practices in this area. The private sector, and, especially, tour operators, could provide information more widely to their clients-the tourists-about tourism and biodiversity issues, and encourage them to conserve, and avoid adverse impact on, biodiversity and cultural heritage to respect national legislation of the visited country, as well as traditions of indigenous and local communities of that country, and to support actions in conformity with the present Guidelines.

87. Awareness campaigns explaining the link between cultural diversity and biological diversity will need to be tailored for various audiences, particularly stakeholders including consumers of tourism, developers and tourism operators.

88. Education and awareness-raising is required at all levels of government. This should include processes for increasing mutual understanding between relevant ministries, including joint and innovative approaches for dealing with tourism and environmental issues.

89. Awareness should also be increased within and outside government that vulnerable ecosystems and habitats are often located within lands and waters occupied or used by indigenous and local communities.

90. The tourism sector as a whole, along with tourists should be encouraged to minimize any negative impacts and maximize positive impacts on biodiversity and local cultures associated with their consumption choices and behaviour, for example through voluntary initiatives.

91. It is also important to raise awareness within the academic sector responsible for training and research on issues regarding the interaction between biological diversity and sustainable tourism, of the role that they can play concerning public education, capacity-building and awareness-raising on these issues.

92. Capacity-building activities should aim to develop and strengthen the capacities of Governments and all stakeholders to facilitate the effective implementation of the present Guidelines, and may be necessary at local, national, regional and international levels.

93. Capacity-building activities can be identified through the adaptive management process and can include strengthening human resources and institutional capacities, the transfer of know-how, the development of appropriate facilities, and training in relation to biological diversity and sustainable tourism issues, and in impact assessment and impact management techniques.

94. Such activities should include ensuring that local communities are equipped with the necessary decision-making abilities, skills and knowledge in advance of future tourist in-flows, as well as with relevant capacity and training regarding tourism services and environmental protection.

95. Capacity-building activities should include, but not be limited to:

   a. Capacity-building and training to assist all stakeholders, including Governments, and indigenous and local communities, in accessing, analysing and interpreting baseline information, undertaking impact assessments and evaluations, impact management, decision-making, monitoring and adaptive management;

b. Development or strengthening of mechanisms for impact assessment with the participation of all stakeholders, including for the approval of the approach, content and scope of impact assessment;

c. Establishment of multi-stakeholder processes involving government departments, tourism sector, non-governmental organizations, indigenous and local communities and other stakeholders;

d. Training of tourism professionals in conservation and biodiversity issues.

96. Information exchange and collaboration regarding sustainable tourism implementation through networking and partnerships between all stakeholders affected by, or involved in tourism, including the private sector, should be encouraged.

5

Tourism in Protected Areas

Tourism has become a major sector of economic activity since the latter part of the twentieth century and all indications are that it will continue growing in the years to come. With this growth, a diversification of tourism products and destinations is taking place, with increased demand for nature-related tourism, including ecotourism, visitation to national and natural parks, rural-based tourism, and the like. The tourists themselves are becoming increasingly sophisticated in their demands; this is not only in terms of luxury at the various establishments they use, but especially in terms of having a meaningful travel experience, including such aspects as cultural authenticity, contacts with local communities, and learning about flora, fauna, special ecosystems and natural life in general, and its conservation.

The expected growth and the new trends observed put tourism in a strategic position to make a positive contribution to, or to negatively affect, the sustainability of natural protected areas and the development potential of surrounding areas and their communities. Tourism can in fact be a major tool for the conservation of such areas and for raising the environmental awareness of residents and visitors. These objectives can be achieved through the generation of financial resources from tourism that can be dedicated to conservation measures, and through appropriate information, interpretation and education programmes for visitors and residents. Additionally, tourism operations within protected areas need to be carefully planned, managed and monitored in order to ensure their long-term sustainability. Otherwise, negative impacts will be generated and tourism will instead contribute to the further deterioration of these areas.

A protected area can be identified as an area of land and/or sea especially dedicated to the protection and maintenance of biological diversity, and of natural and associated cultural resources, and managed through legal or other effective means. In many countries tourism plays a major role in the establishment of protected areas and an area's tourism potential is an important factor in the selection process. No matter what sort of protection an area enjoys, the danger that tourism will harm the natural and aesthetic value of the area is always present.

Tourism activity in a national park or any other protected area can serve as a self-financing mechanism and therefore as a tool of conservation. This will, however, only be possible if the level, type and management of tourism are appropriate and, in particular, the "carrying capacity" of the area is respected.

IUCN has made a distinction in the following six categories of protected areas:

Category	Description
I	Strict Nature Reserve/Wilderness Area: Protected area managed mainly for science or wilderness protection.
Ia	Strict Nature Reserve: Protected area managed mainly for science.
Ib	Wilderness Area: Protected area managed mainly for wilderness protection.
II	National Park: Protected area managed mainly for ecosystem protection and recreation.

III	Natural Monument: Protected area managed mainly for conservation of specific natural features.
IV	Habitat/Species Management Area: Protected area managed mainly for conservation through management intervention.
V	Protected Landscape/Seascape: Protected area managed mainly for landscape/seascape conservation and recreation.
VI	Managed Resource Protected Area: Protected area managed mainly for the sustainable use of natural ecosystems.

Protected areas are a cultural artefact, and have a long history. For example, some historians claim that areas were specifically set aside in India for the protection of natural resources over two millennia ago. In Europe, some areas were protected as hunting grounds for the rich and powerful nearly 1,000 years ago. Moreover, the idea of protection of special places is universal: it occurs among the traditions of communities in the Pacific and parts of Africa, for example.

While many societies set aside special areas for cultural and resource uses, protected areas were first set aside by kings and other national rulers in Europe early in the Renaissance, typically as royal hunting reserves. Slowly these sites became open for public use, providing the basis for community involvement and tourism. The English poet, William Wordsworth, wrote in 1810 of his vision of the Lake District as "a sort of national property".

In 1832, the American poet, explorer, and artist George Catlin pointed to the need for "...a nation's park, containing man and beast, in all the wild and freshness of their nature's beauty". Catlin was responding to the destruction of aboriginal peoples and cultures in the rapidly developing eastern part of this expanding country; in contrast, he perceived a harmony between the native peoples and their environment on the Great

Plains. In 1864, with the Yosemite Grant, the US Congress gave a small but significant part of the present Yosemite National Park to the State of California for "public use, resort and recreation". The first true national park came in 1872 with the dedication of Yellowstone by United States law "as a public park or pleasuring ground for the benefit and enjoyment of the people". Interestingly, the creation of Yellowstone did not allow for the sympathetic treatment of native people and their environment as envisaged by Catlin.

These and other early United States national parks, such as Grand Canyon and Mount Rainier, were created in the west and covered extensive tracts of land with superb natural features. However, the idea of making the great natural areas of the US into national parks was most popular with large sections of the population that lived in the east of the country.

In 1866, the British Colony of New South Wales in Australia reserved 2,000ha (nearly 5,000 acres) of land, containing the Jenolan Caves west of Sydney, for protection and tourism. Later additions created a park complex now known as the Blue Mountains National Park. In 1879, Royal National Park was set up, also in New South Wales, in the wilds south of Sydney, so as to provide a natural recreation area for the burgeoning populations of this metropolitan area.

In 1885, Canada gave protection to hot springs in the Bow Valley of the Rocky Mountains, an area later named Banff National Park. The legislation passed in 1887 borrowed from the Yellowstone legislative wording: the park was "reserved and set aside as a public park and pleasure ground for the benefit, advantage and enjoyment of the people of Canada". The railway companies, whose lines were under development across the country, saw the creation of a park as an excellent way to stimulate passenger growth through tourism

Elsewhere, several forest reserves were set up in South Africa in the last years of the nineteenth century. In 1894, Tongariro National Park was established in New Zealand by agreement with the Maori people, a place that was, and still is, important to them for spiritual reasons.

There were common features to these emerging national parks. First, they were created by government action. Second, the areas set aside were generally large and contained relatively natural environments. Third, the parks were made available to all people. Thus, from the very beginning, park visitation and tourism were central pillars of the national parks movement.

In large, federated countries, such as Australia, Canada, South Africa and the USA, the provincial or state tier of governments also started to create protected areas. For example, the Province of Ontario in Canada created Queen Victoria Niagara Falls Park in 1885 and Algonquin National Park, later named Algonquin Provincial Park, in 1893. As more and more parks were created, it became necessary to set up a coordinated management structure. In 1911, Canada created the world's first park agency, the Dominion Parks Bureau under its director, James B. Harkin. The US National Park Service (USNPS) was established in 1916. The management philosophy given to the USNPS involved both protection and use. The Act states that:

> "the Service thus established shall promote and regulate the use of Federal areas known as national parks, monuments and reservations ... by such means and measures as [to] conform to the fundamental purpose of the said parks, monuments and reservations, which purpose is to conserve the scenery and the natural and historic objects and the wild life therein and to provide for the enjoyment of the same in such manner and by such means as will leave them unimpaired for the enjoyment of future generations".

Both Stephen T. Mather, the first Director of the USNPS and James B. Harkin advocated getting people into the parks so that they could enjoy their benefits and support the parks financially. They also developed management principles and structures to handle such visitation, sometimes creating situations that were later widely regretted.

Thus, a theme that runs right through the early history of protected areas is of people and land together, of people being as much a part of the concept as the land and natural and cultural resources. It was also part of the message of John Muir, Scots émigré and founder of the Sierra Club, who, in his "make the mountains glad" appeal, invited people to get out of the cities and into his beloved Sierra Nevada mountains for the good of their souls. It was also apparent that, almost from the outset, different countries were ready to learn from each other about how to set up and run parks.

So the modern protected area movement has nineteenth century origins in the then "new" nations of Australia, Canada, New Zealand, South Africa and the USA, but during the twentieth century the idea spread around the world. The result was a remarkable expansion in the number of protected areas. Nearly every country passed protected area legislation and designated sites for protection. In all, by the year 2002 some 44,000 sites met the IUCN definition of a protected area; together these covered nearly 10% of the land surface of the planet.

As the network grew, understanding of what is meant by a "protected area" evolved. Thus, the initial, relatively simple concept of large wild areas "set aside" for protection and enjoyment was complemented by other models more appropriate to different parts of the world. Many countries placed more emphasis on cultural values than was initially the case with the early national parks. Protection of lived-in landscapes, for example, came initially from European experience. Also concern with the marine environment has grown markedly in recent years.

The thinking behind the establishment of protected areas developed rapidly too. For example, the development of the science of ecology led in the 1960s to a broader understanding of the need for a systematic approach to resource planning and management. This can be seen with the IUCN classification system for protected areas, which takes biodiversity conservation as its starting point, though it also recognises the importance of other protected area objectives such as recreation and tourism.

Many park systems started to use ecology as the co-ordinating concept for the establishment of new parks. However, when the best and most interesting natural and cultural sites in a country are placed in a protected area framework, there is a natural tendency for people to want to experience these environments. Tourism grew in many parks and became a major element in the culture of society.

Economics was an important consideration in the development of many protected areas. In particular, the economic impact of tourism in protected areas emphasises their community, regional and national importance. It is probable that in the coming decades a developing understanding of the economic impact of park tourism will lead to a more systematic treatment of park tourism. The time may come when a park system is understood within the framework of a park tourism system as well as an ecological system.

Moreover, there is increasing appreciation of the economic importance that many protected areas play by providing environmental services, like water supply, flood control and mitigation of the effects of climate change.

Furthermore, particularly since the adoption of the Convention on Biological Diversity (CBD) in 1992, and especially because of Article 8a, much more stress is now put upon the idea of developing national systems of protected areas as a means of conserving biodiversity in situ and for other purposes. Indeed many protected areas now form part of international networks, both global systems, notably World Heritage sites, Ramsar sites and Biosphere Reserves; and regional systems, such as the Europa 2000 network of nature conservation sites in Europe. There are also calls to recognise fully the role of indigenous peoples in respect of protected areas, and to develop international co-operation in protected areas across national boundaries.

So the notion of protected areas developed a great deal in recent years and now embodies many different ideas. Nonetheless, IUCN has agreed upon a single definition of a protected area as follows:

> "An area of land and/or sea especially dedicated to the protection and maintenance of biological diversity, and of natural and associated cultural resources, and managed through legal or other effective means"

Within this broad IUCN definition, protected areas are in fact managed for many different purposes.

Tourism Planning for Protected Areas

Planning is a process that involves selecting a desirable future out of a range of plausible alternatives, and implementing strategies and actions that will achieve the desired outcome. Thus, by definition, planning moves us from the present to the future. It is critical therefore that planners and tourism operatives understand social, political and economic trends, as these form the context for planning. Such understanding provides opportunities to capitalise on emerging markets, develop actions that are more efficient and effective, and ensure that strategies and actions can be adapted to changing conditions. Since the world is more dynamic than static, park planners and tourism operators need to understand how dynamic change, often non-linear in character, may affect their plans and aspirations.

The growth of interest in sustainable tourism and ecotourism reflects a rising tide of social concern about the quality of the natural environment and the effects of tourism. Activities closely associated with experiencing natural environments are very popular.

Some trends complement each other. Some operate at the global level, some at the local level. Many represent collisions in powerful, but countervailing values and attitudes. Thus, while the trends briefly discussed below are presented independently, one can expect them to interact in various ways, often with unanticipated consequences.

Rising educational levels and demand for travel: The average level of formal educational attainment is rising globally, for both males and females. Literacy is increasing too, particularly in less developed countries. Higher education levels are strongly correlated with demand for outdoor recreation activities, and lead to changes in the patterns of recreation and tourism. As a result, there is a general trend towards appreciative activities, with more travellers seeking life-enriching travel experiences.

There is growth in general interest tourism that involves learning-while-travelling (e.g. guided tours), in specific learning travel programmes (e.g. group educational tours), and generally in learning activities, such as wildlife viewing, attending festivals, cultural appreciation and nature study. The natural and cultural resources found in protected areas, lend themselves to such forms of tourism. And thus the groups most interested in visiting protected areas, such as eco-tourists, tend to be more highly educated than tourists in general.

Tourism of this kind requires explanatory materials (e.g. guides, booklets), interpretive facilities and interpretive guiding (e.g. ecotours). It increases the expectations of service quality in protected areas, and raises political pressure for greater protection of cultural and natural heritage. It can also help generate a greater personal commitment to park protection - something that protected area managers should foster and tap into.

Ageing population: Advances in health care mean that people are living longer. Over the last century, there has been a significant increase in the proportion of people over the age of 60. This proportion is expected to increase even more dramatically over the next century. UN predictions are for 22.1% of the global population to be over 60 in 2050, and 28.1% in 2100. Therefore the proportion of the population which is available to visit protected areas will have an increasingly elderly profile in the future.

Older individuals are staying healthier longer. Although physical capacity decreases with age, older people are increasingly able to lead healthy, physically active lives. So, while the demand for such activities as downhill skiing or mountain climbing decreases with age, elderly people maintain, or even extend, their interest in other outdoor activities, such as walking, nature study, fly-fishing or wildlife observation. Or again, a reduced demand for camping is offset by a greater demand for more comfortable lodge accommodation.

In wealthy countries, the ageing population, early retirement and good savings create large numbers of able-bodied senior citizens with strong inclination to travel. The recreation vehicle industry in the US sells over US $6 billion worth of new vehicles each year, much of it purchased by retirees. This kind of travel is expected to grow in North America, Europe and Australia in the coming decades of this new century.

Older visitors present some challenges for protected area planning and management. For example, there will be a need for more accessible toilets and for trails with lesser gradients; also for greater provision for people with disabilities. On the other hand, older visitors represent an opportunity. They tend to be more interested in the kinds of experience offered by protected areas, have more disposable income, and are thus more willing to pay for higher levels of interpretation, guiding and other services. Park managers must develop an understanding of the needs of this older population, or risk losing the involvement and support of an influential group.

Changing roles of women: In many countries, there has been a revolution in the role of women, and the process continues. More and more, men and women are adopting each other's characteristic role in the workplace and in the household. Women are becoming more prominent, even numerically dominant, in the paid workforce. Often their earnings are increasing more rapidly than those of men; and they make a greater demand for recreation and tourism opportunities. Indeed, it is often women who determine the choice of travel destination.

There are differences between the interests of men and women at the individual activity level. While there are, of course, many exceptions, men tend to be more interested in physically challenging activities, and women tend to be interested in more appreciative activities, such as nature and culture studies and ecotourism.Many women are interested in protected area recreation opportunities. Also, women are increasingly drawn to protected area and tourism management as a career. In many countries, they are moving into key positions in the development of economic, social, environmental and protected area policy.

It is important for protected area managers to understand that the role of women in park travel is strongly influenced by their life stage. Thus single, young women are not generally strong users of protected areas, but women with young children often choose parks as good places for child-centred leisure. Middle aged women often find work and family responsibilities very challenging, leaving them little time for park visitation, an activity requiring planning and considerable time commitment. Older, retired women, especially those travelling with their partners, show strong interest in the activities which involve visiting protected areas.

Changes in the distribution of leisure time: There are important and sometimes conflicting trends in the amounts, distribution and availability of leisure time, a very complex area to understand. For many people, leisure time is increasing due to a shorter working week, increases in the automation of housework and other factors. Yet leisure time is decreasing for others; for example working women who retain household responsibilities. Growth in single parent family numbers increases the leisure time of the absent parent, yet reduces that of the responsible parent. Often young people need to work to support their education, or expand their purchasing power, so they have less leisure time.

Of relevance to park visitation is the re-apportionment of time for vacations. In North America, there tend to be more frequent, shorter vacations, closer to home, rather than two or three week family vacations: short, fast trips (particularly 2 to 4 day weekend trips) now account for 80% of vacation travel in the USA. Therefore many parks now need to allow for short visits by tourists with limited time, which calls for higher quality service, and specialized recreation opportunities. In much of Europe, by contrast, leisure time involves longer paid vacations and shorter working weeks.

For example, Germany introduced a 6-week holiday with pay in the 1990s; and France has adopted a statutory 35-hour week. As a result, European countries, and those of the EU especially, are very important generators of park visitation all over the world. In some of the emerging economies of East Asia, notably China, the advent of paid holidays and greater freedom to travel are creating a fast growing mass market for tourism; as these new tourists become more discriminating, a significant proportion of them are likely to be drawn to protected areas.

Importance of service quality: Tourists are increasingly demanding high quality recreational opportunities and the services that support them. Those who receive quality service during their normal working week expect to be offered this by their leisure providers as well. They expect guides to be knowledgeable and good communicators. They want their hosts to make them feel welcome, comfortable and part of the communities they visit. Increased ecotourism means greater demand for specialised recreation and accommodation, all with a focus on quality.

Most park agencies do not have service quality goals, or monitoring programmes, making their programmes appear unresponsive and primitive. Protected area managers and the private sector need to deliver quality visitor services. The challenges for managers include ensuring they have service quality goals, programmes to deliver high quality service and monitoring programmes in place. Importantly these sophisticated consumers recognise quality service and are willing to pay handsomely for it.

Changing leisure patterns: At first sight, one might expect gains in leisure time to occur in all countries that experience economic development, increased income, ageing populations and the shifting roles of men and women. However, the experience of the more developed countries suggests that in fact some significant losses in leisure timemay occur during the working period of life, particularly among white-collar occupations with very high workloads. But, by contrast, there are big increases in leisure time due to earlier retirement and longer life spans. Older, retired people are also able to travel for longer periods each year.

Rising incomes in North America, Europe, Australia and some parts of Asia in particular are driving up the volume of domestic tourism, and of outbound traffic from these countries. If this continues, there is likely to be a further general increase in recreation pressures upon all protected areas, even remote ones, and of demands for higher quality service.

Advances in global communications and information technology: Among wealthier societies at any rate, many people are now getting access to a huge volume of information on protected areas and travel options through the Internet and other communication technologies. The Internet leads to increased demand for trips to a wider variety of locations, and enables park agencies to provide current, sophisticated information directly to visitors, at very low cost. Since images on the Internet can create expectations about a particular protected area, protected area managers and tourism operators need to be aware of what is being communicated, and to be ready to meet the expectations that have been raised.

These new technologies enable visitors to be well informed about everything, from management policies to the recreation experience. As a result, visitors may be more likely to support protected area policy. However, many protected area agencies, especially those in the developing world, are not yet able to maintain sophisticated Internet web sites. Instead, private interests, such as non-governmental organisations (NGOs), hotel and lodge providers, and tourism companies, provide most of the Internet information. This is particularly so in much of Eastern and Southern Africa, and in South America. When this happens, the protected area agency has little control over the accuracy of information, and cannot influence the kinds of visitor expectations that may be created. Nor can it build support for park management objectives.

Technology may have far-reaching consequences. For example, local hotels, resorts and so forth can cross-market their web sites with those of nearby protected areas, and so increase the number of short visits by business travellers. Private ecotourism resorts can utilise real time web cam experiences (e.g. of wildlife dramas) to draw visitors from around the world. And visitors themselves can help promote awareness of protected areas by providing web cam information about the park to the world while experiencing the park.

There may also be threats from the new technologies. For example, some lobby groups have designed web sites to look exactly like those of a protected area agency, and thus provide potential visitors with false management perspectives. Also park visitors could have access to sophisticated databases in the field, in real time, connected to geo-referenced mapping. This will give them immediate, accurate information on wildlife locations and distributions, along with maps and photos. They may have more information at their disposal than the local park manager has! This could put the manager at a disadvantage in controlling visitor behaviour. The long-term implications of the advances in global communication and information technology are profound and mostly unknown.

Proliferation of travel options: As the world's fleets of passenger aircraft and cruise ships expand, visitors can travel more efficiently, quickly and further afield. International travel has been growing rapidly in the last few decades. The WTO predicts that international travel will grow at the rate of 4.1% annually between now and the year 2020, mostly from North America, Europe and East Asia. While this trend is likely to continue, it will be affected by such factors as the health of the global economy, security fears due to terrorist activities and regional instability, and the extremes of global climate change. Ultimately, the availability and cost of fuel oil will be an important limitation on long-term travel growth.

The proliferation of long-haul air travel has revolutionised global park visitation, with people seeking out World Heritage Sites, national parks and other protected areas. Indeed, the very existence of a protected area, particularly of a national park, is often a lure for tourists. This trend will continue and in general protected area managers should prepare for more visitors from around the globe. While they will present a challenge in terms of language, culture or knowledge and preconceptions of the protected area, they also represent a good source of income, employment, and ameans to convey cultural and ecological values to a wider world.

Cruise ship travel can be particularly problematic. Because large cruise ships carry so many people, they can cause huge environmental and social impacts very quickly. For example, large numbers of people, many of whom are poorly prepared for a marine park experience, can overwhelm a marine protected area. The threats of cultural and ecological damage are very high if there are insufficient management resources. However, in some locations where smaller, expedition-type cruises visit and are expected, protected area managers actually prefer cruise visitors, since staff can prepare to meet and guide the visitors, who come in manageable group sizes. These cruise ship visitors make fewer demands for onshore facilities, thereby reducing the ecological footprint of tourism infrastructure.

Personal security and safety: More than any other factor, threats to personal security and safety adversely affect tourism demand. The fear of terrorism can affect global travel trends. When regional wars, rebellions and terrorism occur, domestic and international travel falls, and fewer tourists visit protected areas. The effects are felt most in developing countries, where international visitors are often a significant proportion of all visitors. A sense of personal security is also affected by the prevalence of violent crime, petty theft, water quality, disease or bad sanitation.

Dramatic differences exist between countries in their ability to provide acceptable levels of security and safety. This is especially relevant to tourism, since people planning their trips will often compare destinations with such factors in mind. Once a destination achieves a negative reputation, it is very difficult to rebuild visitor confidence; and such negative perceptions of a country will also affect the appeal of its protected areas. Violent attacks on tourists themselves, as have recently taken place in Egypt and Uganda for example, can set back tourism by many years. Leisure travel is a luxury good, people have a wide range of opportunities and they will not travel to areas perceived as unsafe. Indeed, the perception of safety is nearly as important as the reality. Many protected areas have been badly affected by unrealistic security concerns created by misleading media reports and poor geographical knowledge of potential consumers. Managers must expect some naïve visitors who are not prepared for the dangers that occur in many natural environments.

Protected area managers should be aware of safety expectations of visitors, explain the local situation to potential visitors, and respond to visitor safety demands. If possible, protected area managers need to have security management plans in place, including a public relations component. It is important both to take security seriously and to tell people exactly what the situation is. Failure to do so can lead to complicated and expensive results, since it is becoming more common for park visitors to take legal action against park management for safety-related injury, or damage to personal property.

Increasing social and environmental concerns: Across the globe, people express concern about social injustices and environmental problems. They are increasingly aware of the need for low impact tourism which does not harm the environment. They tend to want to support local conservation or community development initiatives. They are themselves moving from consumptive to less consumptive activities, often adopting "green consumer" life styles. The growth of interest in sustainable tourism and ecotourism is a response to such concerns. Protected areas are well placed to take advantage of this trend as they embody the values that such travellers hold. Some tourists are "voting with their feet". They are attracted to destinations that have a positive reputation, and are actively avoiding destinations that have social or environmental problems. There are also international schemes for recognising the adoption of high environmental standards in tourism provision.

Globalisation of the economy: In a globalised economy, individual countries and communities are influenced by decisions and economic conditions elsewhere. Thus political or corporate decisions in origin countries can influence overseas travel, which may in turn affect the viability of protected area tourism a continent away. This linkage between origin and destination communities makes achieving sustainable tourism difficult, since the host country often has a limited ability to influence tourist trends; it also leads to competition between destinations. However, protected area managers can take advantage of this global context through clever marketing, using the Internet and by promoting the distinctive niche which they offer as a tourist destination. To do this, protected area agencies should have knowledge of global tourism trends, so as to position themselves, develop the right messages, and respond through appropriate management measures.

Diversification of Tourism Markets

The number of people taking part in many outdoor activities is growing, especially in hiking, cycling and water-based activities such as sea kayaking or scuba diving. There has also been a huge growth in 'soft' adventure and ecotourism or nature-tourism types of trips. 'Soft' activities are those where a more casual, less dedicated approach is taken to the activity or natural attraction, and a desire to experience it with some basic degree of comfort; whereas 'hard' adventure or ecotourism involves specialist interest or dedicated activity, and a willingness to experience the outdoors or wilderness with few comforts. The tourism industry has responded to this range of interests by developing many types of niche market packages.

Protected areas are very attractive settings for the growing demand for outdoor, appreciative activities in natural environments. Challenges for protected area managers are to ensure that while visitors have opportunities to participate in desired activities, they are aware of and maintain the values. Opportunities are to tap into such market demand, through target market programming, perhaps in collaboration with the private sector, both to increase attractiveness as a destination, and manage the visitors appropriately.

There is no such thing as the "average protected area visitor". In reality, markets comprise many segments, each of which has somewhat different characteristics, expectations, activity participation and spending patterns. Marketing exploits these visitor segments by comparing and matching them with the biophysical and cultural attributes of the park, and then sensitively promoting appropriate protected area attributes to the targeted segment. This reduces adverse impacts on the protected area, increases the economic benefits and makes it more likely that visitors are satisfied.

Ways to segment visitors include:

1) *By socio-demographic characteristics*: Thus, one segment might be those under 30, while another might be visitors of 65 and older. These segments would be expected to have different characteristics and activity participation.

2) *By geographic characteristics*: Thus one market may be local visitors, whereas another might be international travellers.

3) *By "psychographic" segments:* Thus, one segment might be considered "escapers" who look for adventure, and getting away from it all, while another might be considered "green" and actively seeking environmentally-sensitive products and services.

4) *By activity participation:* Thus, one segment might be "tent campers" while another might be "wildlife

viewers". This method is easy, because the segments are easily identifiable. However, it should be noted that one visitor might engage in a number of activities. Each segment has different expectations of what they desire from an area.

5) *By frequency of participation*: Thus, one segment may be "frequent travellers" or "repeat visitors"; another "first-time visitors". Frequent travellers and repeat visitors usually have more informed expectations of the protected area, and may have more involvement and care more about it.

6) *By perceived product benefits:* Thus, one segment might expect to benefit from a challenging environment (e.g. through river floating or mountain climbing), while others might expect to learn about nature. Some might wish to socialise with friends or family, while others might simply expect to enjoy natural beauty. Segments can be identified by the product characteristics they prefer. The value of segmentation is that it can predict behaviour, and thus help managers to plan for this behaviour. Segmentation by perceived product benefit can be used to develop an understanding of what tourists really seek in a visit to a protected area, and so establish an appropriate management response. In this way, visitors will gain greater satisfaction from the products and services offered.

Sophisticated research capabilities and procedures are normally required to understand the market in this way. Hall and McArthur point out that the behaviour of various market segments is best understood when inferred variables (rather than objective variables) are used. Inferred variables are obtained by directly questioning samples of a population (e.g. of visitors) about such things as motivations, expectations and attitudes. For protected area managers without sophisticated research capabilities, the best approach would be a combination of sample surveys and observing how services and facilities are used.

Benefits of Tourism in Protected Areas

Tourism in protected areas produces benefits and costs. These effects interact often in complex ways. It is the responsibility of the protected area planner to maximise benefits while minimising costs. Protected areas are established primarily to preserve some type of biophysical process or condition such as a wildlife population, habitat, natural landscape, or cultural heritage such as a community's cultural tradition. Tourists visit these protected areas to understand and appreciate the values for which the area was established and to gain personal benefits.

Tourism planning and development aims to take advantage of the interest shown by tourists so as to: enhance economic opportunities, protect the natural and cultural heritage, and advance the quality of life of all concerned.

Enhancing economic opportunity

Tourism can increase jobs and income in a local area or region. It is often regarded as a source of foreign exchange, particularly since protected areas tend to attract international tourists. Governments often use tourism for economic development because it is relatively inexpensive to create a tourism job compared to one in manufacturing. To gain such economic benefits, two conditions must be met: (1) there must be products and services for tourists to spend money on, and (2) it is necessary to minimise the amount that leaks out of the local area. "Leakage" can be a serious problem: for example, less than 6% of tourism income at Tortuguero

National Park, Costa Rica, accrues to the local communities. So tourism should be as self-sufficient as possible, reducing dependence on out-of-region goods and services.

While some tourism developments in connection with protected areas will have a large initial cost, they may well generate significant revenues over the longer term. For example, in St. Lucia, most tourist arrivals currently visit the Sulphur Springs National Landmark. If the park were to be enhanced, estimates of costs and revenues show that not only would these costs be recovered, but also so would the costs of adding staff, programming, facilities and maintenance. The estimated costs were expected to outweigh the estimated revenues for the first two years but, thereafter, benefits would exceed costs.

Tourism income from popular protected areas can be used to help finance others that cannot attract so many tourists, or where large numbers would be inappropriate. Conservation revenues may actually be higher than other land use revenues. For example, in the Devure Ranch in Zimbabwe, Pricewaterhouse Cooper estimated that cattle had the potential to generate Z $22/hectare/year, using a realistic stocking rate. By contrast, a small wildlife tourism operation could generate Z$67/ hectare/year . However, the Zimbabwe Government decided that land resettlement of local people was a more important objective.

In the last few years most wildlife tourism operations in that country have ceased to be viable, due to a loss of land for conservation and to a decline in the number of tourists. Both the Rwanda and Zimbabwe examples illustrate that civil unrest impacts tourism, and the positive economic benefits of tourism, very strongly. Leisure travel is a luxury good, and people have a wide range of opportunities.

Therefore, they will not travel to areas which they perceive as unsafe. Protected area managers should aim to develop tourism development policies which support long-term economic development and encourage repeat visits. They should try to maximise local employment, social and cultural benefits through high visitor spending and low local leakage.

Guidelines for capturing economic benefits are:

— *Increase the number of visitors*: Increasing visitation is risky unless the financial benefits from the visitors exceed their costs. It may increase other impacts, some negatively.

— *Increase the length of stay*: Increased length of stay provides more opportunity to sell local products and services.

— *Attract richer market niches:* Different marketing tactics may bring in consumers with strong abilities to spend.

— Increase purchases per visitor: Offering more locally-made goods for sale, available directly and indirectly to the visitor, helps increase visitor expenditure and local incomes.

— *Provide lodging*: The costs of overnight accommodation are relatively large and are paid for locally. Local lodging also increases expenditures on meals, and local goods and services.

— *Provide guides or other services:* Since much tourist activity in protected areas is information intensive, there are usually good opportunities for guide services.

— *Host events*: Artwork, crafts and festivals based on local culture can increase local economic impact.

— *Purchase local food and drink*: When visitors, park staff and tourism employees consume locally grown food and drink, they provide important income to local farmers.

Some leakage of expenditure to sources outside the local area is unavoidable, simply because not all food, supplies and services are produced locally. However, tourism planners should try to minimise this leakage. Whatever the strategy employed, it is important that local communities are involved in planning for the economic impacts and how they should be measured.

Protecting natural and cultural heritage

Tourism based on protected areas can be a key factor in supporting the conservation of the natural and cultural heritage. It can generate the funds through entrance and service fees, local taxes and in many other ways that can be used directly to help meet or offset the costs of conservation, maintaining cultural traditions and providing education.

Indirectly, by demonstrating the economic value that protected area tourism can bring to a country or a region, it can build public and political support for conservation of natural heritage. Tourism enables some marine protected areas to prosper, for example in the Netherlands Antilles (Bonaire Marine Park), the Seychelles (Ste. Anne National Marine Park) and Kenya (Malindi/Watamu parks and reserves). There are many thousands of other examples of such positive relationships between conservation of biodiversity and the natural environment, and protected areas-based tourism.

Well-managed tourism can also assist in protecting or restoring a community's or a region's cultural heritage. Protected areas have an important part to play in respect of the built heritage. Many protected areas contain significant historic, architectural and archaeological resources. Tourism can provide income to help in the upkeep or repair of such important buildings and landscape features. It may be collected directly, for example through entry or user fees or indirectly through local taxes.

The cultural heritage is also evident in local traditions. Tourists sometimes seek authentic experiences. It may therefore be possible to encourage the local community to maintain or re-establish important cultural festivals, traditions or events, and even to undertake the restoration of heritage buildings. There are many benefits from such activities. They will enrich the tourism experience within or near protected areas, thereby inducing tourists to stay longer and spend more.

Exposure to cultural diversity can help modify tourist behaviour, change use patterns and create advocates for conservation among the tourist community. Moreover local communities may benefit when local traditions and values are maintained, and when they are encouraged to take greater pride in their communities or regions.

Enhancing quality of life in the host community

Tourism development should be designed to protect what is good about a host community and tackle those aspects that need to be improved. One way in which this can be done is to develop facilities and services for tourism which can also benefit the living conditions of local residents. Indeed protected areas can be the engines of sustainable rural development. IUCN advises that protected areas in Africa should be repositioned "in the context of community development and the local economy". It argues that protected areas, sustained by tourist income, not only create jobs and raise income but can also be used to support local communities' needs for:

— *Improved communications:* upgrading roads for tourism access gives neighbouring villages better access to the outside world. Telecommunications access to protected area offices can be vital to local communities in times of emergency;

— *Education*: some protected areas provide language, literacy and numeracy training to their staff, skills than can then be applied in the community as well;

— *Training*: the training that parks staff receive in such matters as vehicle maintenance or food hygiene will be of practical use in local communities;

— *Health care*: the medical services available to parks staff and visitors can be shared with local communities.

Thus tourism to terrestrial and marine protected areas may be viewed as a tool to help communities to maintain, or improve, their living standards and quality of life. This may be measured in terms of:

— increased school graduation rates;

— reduced infant mortality;

— elimination of water and air pollution;

— increased access to recreation sites, protected areas or subsistence resources; and

— better access to services, such as the park's programmes for interpretation and environmental education, which also benefit locals.

Protected areas can also be used to enhance the quality of life of a whole nation, by making them the foundation of a national policy to raise environmental understanding.

Risks of Tourism in Protected Areas

Negative effects can and do result from tourist visitation, but many of them can be competently managed and alleviated. Protected area stakeholders are in the position of gauging both the positive and negative effects of tourism, determining how acceptable the negative effects are, and suggesting how they can be managed. The costs of tourism are of three kinds: financial and economic, socio-cultural and environmental.

Economic costs

Tourism brings increased demand for goods, services and facilities, such as lodging, restaurants, other attractions, and personal vacation properties. As visitor numbers increase, so do the demands for basic services such as policing, fire, safety and health care. Such increased demand brings increased costs and possibly higher tax burdens for the local community. In some cases, costs may rise so much that local residents can no longer afford to live there. This is particularly the case in destinations where local people have lower incomes than the visitors do. For example, wealthy foreign visitors to protected areas in developing countries may see economic opportunities and take control or buy out local businesses. Thus tourism can lead to increased foreign ownership and raised property values.

Increased visitation also means increased costs to the protected area management agency as it strives to add the additional personnel and facilities needed by the tourists. This cost of tourism must be weighed against the benefits. Therefore, the park agency must be able to apply the benefits earned from tourists against the costs. As already noted, where the local economy and protected areas are heavily dependent on tourism, they may become vulnerable to external factors beyond their control, such as natural disasters, currency fluctuations, competitive capture of markets or political instability.

Some leakage of tourist expenditures will occur, whether it is out of the protected area, local community, region or the country. If local people do not benefit, they may look for other more profitable activities and land uses. Hence the need to minimise leakage.

Social costs

Increased numbers of tourists may disturb community activities, and compete for recreation places and other services. Poorly planned tourism development can lead to increased congestion, littering, vandalism and crime. Governments may exacerbate these problems if they put short-term economic considerations before all else, for example by building inappropriate infrastructure or failing to establish the needs of local communities. When this happens, the local support for the protected area may be put at risk.

Sometimes tourism in protected areas calls only for seasonal employment, leaving residents underemployed during the slow or off-seasons. However, this may be to the local communities' liking. In the Klondike Gold Rush National Historic Park (Alaska, USA) the entire town of Skagway revolves around summer tourism. In the winter, many people leave, and then the community apparently enjoys its "quiet time", having earned sufficient income for the year during the busy season.

Where protected area agencies develop visitor management regulations that also affect local residents, there may be negative socio-cultural impacts (e.g. prohibitions on traditional uses such as fuelwood gathering or on spiritual uses which require entry to the protected area). Other negative impacts may occur where local traditions become commercialized, and lose their integrity or authenticity. An example would be dances, which had once had a vital social role but which are now put on only for the entertainment of visitors.

Negative impacts are most common when communities are not given choices, or have no control over their involvement with tourism. Outsiders often assign negative connotations to cultural change, while those undergoing the change may be positive about the new ideas or approaches. So it is important that those affected by cultural change be the ones that decide whether this change is acceptable.

Appropriate planning is needed ahead of development, to avoid adverse impacts from the outset; but there are also management techniques that can be used to address problems should they arise. The dangers are all the greater when there is a sharp contrast between the wealth of tourists and the poverty of the host community. Where this occurs, local communities are potentially vulnerable to exploitation and their voice may go unheard. Both the protected area manager and the tourist provider have a special responsibility in such circumstances to ensure that the community is listened to, and its views allowed to help shape the form of tourist development that takes place.

Environmental costs

Tourism, like many other forms of development, will always produce environmental impacts, even at low levels of intensity, and despite the best efforts of protected area managers. Such impacts occur both at the site level, and over larger areas. Because tourism in protected areas is drawn to environments which are inherently sensitive, it is vital that the impacts be assessed as accurately as possible beforehand to establish if they are acceptable. Ecotourism and sustainable tourism strategies are designed to manage park visitation to maximize positive benefits and minimise negative environmental impacts prior to their occurrence. This is best achieved through well-designed planning strategies.

A key issue is to be sensitive to cumulative impacts, to practice adaptive management, and to achieve consensus among stakeholders about how much impact is acceptable, and where, in the protected area.

Tourism in Privately-owned Protected Areas

In IUCN's protected area category system, areas may be publicly-owned, privately-owned, owned by the community or owned by amixture of some or all of these possibilities. Management may be equally diverse. In some parts of the world, privatelyowned conservation lands are becoming a significant force for both conservation and tourism, and are flourishing. Such areas include privately-owned parks, NGO reserves, private hunting reserves, and biological and research stations run by universities.

Tourism at private nature reserves varies from large resorts with a reserve as an added attraction, to small ecolodges within large nature reserves. Private reserves are often found adjacent to or nearby major public parks. Also, particularly in Category V and VI protected areas, there are extensive tracts of privately-owned land which are farmed or otherwise managed for resource use, but which are important for their contribution to landscape protection and biodiversity conservation. Another rapidly growing area is that of indigenous, aboriginal and community-owned protected areas.

Several forces are at work here, including: political empowerment of previously marginalised groups; devolution of power from central gov-ernment; greater use of the private sector to deliver public services; and the desire of individuals, commercial operations and communities to benefit from the economic activity generated by tourism.

The growing trend towards private ownership of protected areas was explained by a greater public interest generally in biodiversity protection, governments' inability to safeguard all biodiversity, and the expansion in ecotourism. Also, some communities have developed communally managed reserves to generate income in ways that are compatible with their lifestyle.

Tourism may be viewed as a way of financing conservation activities, as a means of making money, or as a more favourable alternative to some other form of land use. Whatever the reasons, the reality is that, in many parts of both the developed and developing world, the initiative for setting up protected areas is no longer coming only or even mainly from central government. As a result, tourism in protected areas is no longer just about an activity affecting publicly-owned and publicly-managed land.

Private reserves play an important role in Costa Rica, a country that has enjoyed political stability and has stable land ownership laws. An extensive system of both public and private reserves supports an ecotourism industry. There is a long tradition that links the scientific researchers and ecotourism. The ecological research highlighted the importance of Costa Rica's tropical ecosystems, leading to increased demand for protection and ecotourism.

Researchers established many of the private reserves, which are run more efficiently than those managed by government agencies, are able to respond quickly to the market, and are able to generate resources to support other types of conservation and development activities.

The average extent of private reserves in Costa Rica is small, and most owners are more concerned with quality of management than with size of the reserve.

Profit is often a secondary consideration for reserve owners. Many of them value conservation and land stewardship more highly, and over 75% of owners placed bequest value very highly.

However, a few private reserves are quite large, such as the impressive Monteverde Cloud Forest Reserve. Africa has had a long tradition of using private and community lands for tourism to supplement other activities. For example, until recently the CAMPFIRE communal areas management programme for indigenous resources in Zimbabwe generated 90% of its income from trophy hunting, with the remainder coming from photographic safaris, hides and ivory sales and other tourist-related activities. Similar community-based tourism is flourishing in Namibia.

In 1989, in 63 private reserves in Latin America and Africa, tourism accounted for 40% of operating income. By 1993, this had increased to 67% of the reserves' operating income. Approximately half of the respondents depended on tourism for 90% or more of their income, and just over one third were completely dependent on it.

South Africa has thousands of private game reserves, each with its own mix of wildlife conservation and tourism. Many sell trophy hunting and harvest wildlife meat for sale. These reserves tend to provide high-cost visitor services, while leaving the more inexpensive operations to the national and provincial park services. In South Africa, as elsewhere, many private reserves are located near national parks. For example, much of the west side of Kruger National Park is buttressed by adjacent private game reserves. The land in these reserves adds considerably to the area and conservation value of the entire ecosystem.

Many reserves are owned and managed by NGOs, mainly for biodiversity conservation, both in developing and developed countries. For example, The Program for Belize owns and manages the Rio Bravo Conservation and Management Area, covering 92,614ha, or approximately 4% of Belize's land area. Ecotourism is the largest single source of funds (45% in 1995) available to meet the costs of running the reserve. The Nature Conservancy of the USA owns more than 1,300 reserves, making it one of the largest private systems of nature sanctuaries in the world. This private organisation recognised the importance of ecotourism to the long-term financial sustainability of protected areas and developed an international programme of planning, guide training, financial research, ecolodge development and business planning to assist private and public reserve managers. The Royal Society for the Protection of Birds (RSPB) in the UK is another large conservation NGO whose conservation achievements have largely been built on the back of visits to its reserves by the public.

Like all protected areas, private reserves are vulnerable to political unrest, poaching, community opposition to loss of access to resources, squatters and sometimes antipathy towards tourism. Private reserves are also very susceptible to fluctuations in the ecotourism market.

Success will depend upon a number of factors, including:

— extensive community involvement at the outset and subsequently;

— a non-forced negotiating position between parties;

— a legal framework to allow tourism revenues to be retained by private land managers;

— sufficient revenues from tourism for management, conservation and profits to support the enterprise and contribute to conservation;

— mutual understanding of differing goals between stakeholders;

— an understanding by the managers of the constraints over their operations;

— mechanisms to cover injury liability affecting tourists and residents;

— mechanisms which link public and commercial tourism; and

— commercial tourism being able to focus on heavily visited sites.

The establishment of protected areas and providing for tourism often work best when they come from within the community, even if this is done with outside support from NGOs or government sources.

6

Tourism and Ethical Issues

Tourism is not just an economic transaction or a series of activities which can be isolated from everyday life or from their impact on people. The very fact that tourism involves travel to another culture and direct contact with the people there, raises a number of ethical issues.

Tourism to developing countries is growing and has a disproportionate impact on the poor. They may gain access to the jobs in the industry and receive new opportunities to provide goods and services. However, they also live in the areas which receive the most destructive forms of tourism, thus bearing the brunt without reaping the benefits. The poor suffer the worst effects and they should be the focus of any improvements.

Tourism is not just an economic issue but also a social one as there are numerous contingent relationships established between the buyer and those involved in the production, manufacture, marketing and selling. Tourism is one of the global industries which have the greatest impact on people and it should therefore have their well-being, especially those on the receiving end, as its foundation. The people who live on the land, open up their homes and their lives, and provide services for tourists are those whose concerns should be first.

The tourism industry has a global reach and the potential to make a positive contribution to development. It is also in its best interests to do so, as its success is based on the ability of the people and environment to provide a good service and to ensure the possibility of future use. The industry has gone some way to addressing a few environmental concerns but has been slow to address the social, cultural and economic issues. Initial priorities must be to ensure good working conditions, allow local people to participate in tourism planning and implementation, ensure that a greater share of tourism revenue goes to the host communities and invest in local resources, labour and skills.

Tourists can have significant influence on the industry and if there is sufficient demand for the industry to behave in an ethical way, then the industry will have to respond. In fact, it will be in the industry's best interests to respond to customer concerns. Tourists can also make a positive contribution to development by the way they act when on holiday. This could involve using local services and staying in locally-run guesthouses, treating everyone with respect, learning about and honouring local customs, and looking after the environment.

Increases in international travel by public sector employees and others, along with incidents of terrorism, accidents, and disease, raise a variety of ethical issues not normally covered in the training of public personnel administrators or in the standard administrative ethics course. Issues of accessibility for individuals with disabilities may be familiar to personnel administrators and students of ethics, but take on vast new dimensions when those individuals travel abroad. Travel-related ethics issues involved in health, safety, and accessibility may include identification of individual and institutional responsibilities, informed consent, contingency planning, emergency response mechanisms, fairness, and equal treatment.

Governmental agencies, professional associations, and other institutions have sought to develop effective responses to health, safety, and accessibility challenges arising from rapidly-expanding international travel. Health and safety guidelines, vulnerability assessments, and other ethics strategies will help institutions and administrators to deal with future challenges, but the key task is for administrators at all levels to become more aware of the issues surrounding this, the world's largest industry.

Public personnel are faced with an ethical crisis they scarcely recognize: what to do about international tourism. In 1998 more than 600 million people traveled internationally, a figure that is expected to soar to 1.6 billion by 2020. That kind of growth will put intense pressures on governmental personnel to cope with a wide range of health, security, and accessibility issues. Most nations consider domestic and international tourism to be an important part of their economies with pro-growth efforts expected to be supported by both the public and private sector. Even the United States, which makes a virtue out of the private sector and often a scapegoat out of the public sector, by 1985 had 43 federal agencies dealing in some way with tourism. Every state and all major cities along with hundreds of smaller communities are making elaborate efforts to boost economic growth through tourism. Indeed, tourism is one of the few public sector areas that has not been downsized.

Public sector employees not only boost, manage, budget, monitor, and administer tourist attractions, but they also administer the licensing, taxing, and zoning through which tourism is developed and maintained. Those same employees are also tourists themselves—

dependent at home and abroad on the policies that support their health and safety. Terrorism, accidents, disease, and accessibility problems may be increasing with tourism growth, but not all these threats are borne by the tourists. Balancing visitor and community needs grows more and more difficult. Host populations, local health, transport, and criminal justice facilities may also be taxed by the health-related issues exacerbated by tourism. What is needed? A new level of coordination and commitment by public bodies ranging from the local level to the World Health Organization are essential for meeting the challenge. Yet, there is little evidence of the necessary political will to confront the problems associated with the rapid expansion of tourism. No one builds a career squelching tourism; little credit is given to exposing new problems so that they might be prevented.

Still, it is critical that students of public administration and government employees learn to recognize and confront the host of ethical issues not typically covered in the training of public administrators or in the standard ethics course. In the U.S., for example, issues of accessibility for individuals with disabilities are covered in training about the Americans with Disabilities Act, but not considered generally are U.S. government personnel, tourists, or other travelers going abroad

Partly due to cultural clashes and loss or change in indigenous identity and values that tourism brings about in host destinations, tourism can create more serious situations where ethical and even criminal issues are involved.

Crime Generation

Crime rates typically increase with the growth and urbanisation of an area, and growth of mass tourism is often accompanied by increased crime. The presence of a large number of tourists with a lot of money to spend, and often carrying valuables such as cameras and jewellery, increases the attraction for criminals and brings with it activities like robbery and drug dealing. Repression of these phenomena often exacerbates social tension.

In Rio de Janeiro, Brazil, tourists staying in beachside five star resorts close to extremely poor communities in hillside "favelas" (shantytowns) are at risk of pickpockets and stick-ups. Security agents, often armed with machine guns, stand guard nearby in full sight, and face aggressive reactions from locals who are often their neighbours when they go home. Tourism can also drive the development of gambling, which may cause negative changes in social behaviour.

Child Labour

Studies have shown that many jobs in the tourism sector have working and employment conditions that leave much to be desired: long hours, unstable employment, low pay, little training and poor chances for qualification. In addition, recent developments in the travel and tourism trade (liberalisation, competition, concentration, drop in travel fares, growth of subcontracting) and introduction of new technologies seem to reinforce the trend towards more precarious, flexible employment conditions. For many such jobs young children are recruited, as they are cheap and flexible employees.

Prostitution and Sex Tourism

The commercial sexual exploitation of children and young women has paralleled the growth of tourism in many parts of the world. Though tourism is not the cause of sexual exploitation, it provides easy access to it. Tourism also brings consumerism to many parts of the world previously denied access to luxury commodities and services. The lure of this easy money has caused many young people, including children, to trade their bodies in exchange for T-shirts, personal stereos, bikes and even air tickets out of the country. In other situations children are trafficked into the brothels on the margins of the tourist areas and sold into sex slavery, very rarely earning enough money to escape. A study in Kalutara, Sri Lanka, found that out of 100 schoolchildren 86 children had had their first sexual experience aged 12 or 13, the majority with a foreign tourist.

Political Pressure to Facilitate Tourism

The political pressure to facilitate tourism in the name of economic development over "red tape" that may include protection of both tourist and nontourist. Just as community, state, and national officials are loath to assess the politically useful industry in terms of its costs rather than merely its tax receipts, they also oftentimes lack the political will or the contingency planning effort needed to prevent major problems.

Often the "rational" decision for local bureaucrats is to acquiesce to local demand, though they may foresee a larger, long-term threat to the public interest. Cost-benefit analysis tends to discount the future threat over the present advantage.

The importance of tourism economically and politically has shifted the bureaucrat's constituency to a few economic interests and favors the tourist over the general citizenry. For example, tourist resorts may lack adequate sewage facilities. In the short run, the tourist may be spared dysentery by drinking bottled water. In the long run, however, the communities and villages surrounding the resort may experience polluted wells, unsafe beaches, and a decline in the local fishing industry.

If the public sector seeks to enforce tough standards in the design phase, its inspectors may be bribed or the dangers belittled and the advantages of economic development oversold. Later the resort or attraction may have its own local clout sufficient to control planning. Even when a major health hazard exists as with the medical waste washed up on New Jersey's beaches a few years ago or even where disease and political instability threaten, public officials generally do not dissuade tourists from coming. One of the few exceptions, and that possible only because of the government's authoritarian control, occurred when Marshall Tito, President of Yugoslavia, closed his country's borders in 1975 and forbade travel among towns, successfully "burning out" a smallpox epidemic.

More commonly, public sector tourism organizations promote tourism as being good for the health and a "stressbuster." Some even wink at prostitution by advertising "a fresh peach on every beach" and "Try a Virgin... island." Even where prostitution is prosecuted, which is far from every place it is illegal, there is usually a double standard that leads to prosecution of the prostitute but not the one buying the sexual services. In an era dominated by the AIDS epidemic, such public sector marketing is a disgrace.

Nor are children adequately protected from pedophiles B some of whom actually tour as groups exploiting children. This is a serious problem in many countries, but it is particularly difficult to control in developing countries where low civil service salaries encourage bribery.

Distribution of Police and Judicial Services

Another ethical problem is the distribution of police and judicial services. Affluent travelers are often afforded more protection than nontourists. Some cities have special patrols in the tourist belt. Sentences may be harsher for crimes against tourists. Is this consistent with equal justice? Many would argue it isn't. "Those who have less in life should have more in law," argued former Philippine President, Ramon Magsaysay. Others, however, note the special vulnerability of tourists, often unfamiliar with the destination, its language, signage, money, traffic patterns, or customs. Moreover, on vacation people are more apt to be careless or behave more recklessly than at home.

All of these behaviors set them up for criminals. Hawaii and several other states have taken special efforts to fly tourists back to their state in order to testify against alleged criminals. Enforcement officials say this is necessary to protect tourism and keep tourists from being targeted because they are transients. The motives may not be altogether altruistic, but they might fit John Rawls' dictum on justice, which includes treating everyone equally, except in those instances where the most vulnerable would benefit from unequal treatment.

Health and Safety Issues

International travel is not a new phenomenon. The arrival of widebodied jets in the 1960s democratized travel by making it more affordable. The decolonization of Asia and Africa plus the Cold War also meant increasing numbers of embassies, consulates, and transnational corporations that governments needed to keep secure. Thus, what was once the Grand Tour for the select few became a mass movement of government personnel, business people, tourists, and students- all of concern to their home and host countries.

Health and safety issues are also not new issues in travel. Within a week of the 1912 sinking of the Titanic, policies were passed around the world mandating adequate lifeboats on ocean liners and calling for international monitoring of icebergs. The international community can make ethical judgments to save lives when the attention of the world is clearly focused on the problem.

The 1917-1918 influenza epidemic also served as a cautionary tale of how the movement of travelers B in this case primarily soldiers B could unleash deadly terror on civilian populations and their unprepared governments. Between 20 and 30 million people died, far more than from World War I fighting.

Accessibility for people with disabilities is a relatively new issue and, except in a few nations, has been scarcely addressed. These issues are certain to become more serious and will raise increasingly difficult ethical dilemmas. Whereas travel was once considered a private decision, it is now ringed by government policies on access, promotion, safety, immigration, customs, disease control, and even foreign policy Tourism trends will dramatically accelerate ethical issues for public administrators in all these policy areas.

The first concern is the enormous growth in travel, for which public administrators and policy makers are simply not prepared. More than a 300 percent increase in international travel is expected by 2020. Already over two million people cross international boundaries every day. Domestic tourism will be several times that amount! Crowding exacerbates a desire to get away from it all; so, at the same time tourism is becoming more urban, it is also radically changing once remote settings.

The U.S. national parks are an example. Parking rather than the park itself is becoming the preoccupation of park service personnel. Is this simply a changing role to which personnel must adapt as they encourage access and participation in the once wild parks? Or should employees resist by banning cars or rationing access as a way to protect the larger public interest in preserving a national resource and keeping the quality of the experience special? Cost-benefit analysis does not prepare the administrator adequately for protecting either the longterm integrity of the resource or measuring the quality of the experience unlimited access provides. What other values need to be weighed? A second concern is the global booming senior market. According to the UN, the number of senior citizens in the year 2025 will be 1,100,000,000 B almost double the number estimated for the year 2000 and five times the 1950 figure. Throughout the world we are witnessing 'double demographic aging', a phenomenon in which a longer life span, together with the record decline in birth rates, produces demographic growth rates very close to zero, and in some cases, negative growth.

In the U.S. seniors are 25 percent of the population but control 70 percent of the wealth. They also have disproportionate political clout. Yet their propensity to travel creates extra safety and health concerns, especially when they venture abroad. These concerns are beginning to impact global decision-making bodies. The United Nations declared 1994 the International Year of the Elderly. There is a growing awareness that "a central requirement of any social programme is the principle of the right to useful and worthwhile activity for all. This means that government must draft and implement active policies for training, leisure, and social integration." Currently, little if anything is being done to prepare public sector personnel for participating in tourism development that targets the special needs -particularly health needs-of this group.

Deregulation, privatization, increased industry competitiveness, and the speed of world travel have encouraged pressures to cut corners on safety, especially in terms of food preparation and sanitation. Today, food poisoning and medical emergencies are a far greater threat than crime or terrorism.

A study done by the British Consumers Association revealed that 15 percent of their members had been sick on vacation. Sixty to 75 percent experienced illness when visiting developing nations. These percentages are probably similar for other travelers. The pillows or blankets on planes often harbor lice, mosquitos, fungi, viruses, and germs as the plane moves through airport after airport before getting a thorough cleaning. Dengue fever, TB, hantavirus, malaria, and other diseases are carried around the globe in hours.

Public officials are often faced with increasingly lax policy standards at a time of reduced vigilance by the private sector. Public pressures may also reduce safety: Immigration, agricultural inspectors, and customs officials are sometimes upbraided by U.S. Department of Commerce personnel and members of Congress for their slow handling of inbound planes and ships. The critics remind employees that they must facilitate tourism to boost it. The visitor or returning citizen must not be harassed or delayed. The conscientious employee may be urged to lighten up."

Many ships and planes simply register in countries where restrictions are looser. Allowing the whistle on potential hazards for the traveling public or the host destination is often not an option. Increasingly, concerns are voiced even in the tourist industry press. The World Health Organization, criticized for timidity in the face of member resistance, is also beginning to act. Increasingly, the link between a potential for bioterrorism or even accidental spread of infectious disease has gradually encouraged greater global NGO and public sector cooperation. These trends have highlighted a growing awareness that tourism B once and still promoted as a boon to one's health and the salvation of many a community's tax base B may be a mixed blessing at best

Though an extraordinarily violent nation with extremely expensive health care, the U.S. and its communities are careful only to accentuate the positive. Nor is this practice unusual. The Philippines still includes in its brochures information about areas the unwary would discover were in the midst of a civil war. It is left to the Internet and private guidebooks to provide cautionary advice to the domestic or international tourist.

As an example, Fielding's Guide to Dangerous Places found that Florida was far more dangerous for Europeans than North Africa, Turkey, California, and Kenya, combined. On the other hand, governments are not nearly so loath to warn about other countries. Keeping tourism at home obviously supports a nation's balance of payments, but it is more than that. Developed nations, especially the U.S., Japan and the U.K., are quick to note areas of risk, often with a range of foreign office bulletins ranging from advisories to "don't go" to absolute prohibitions on travel.

The latter are sometimes more political than strictly cautionary. This leads to the dilemma: Should travelers' health and security advisories serve foreign and economic policy? Or does a lack of candor sacrifice government credibility on future, perhaps more important, issues? For those who read the warnings and don't go abroad, credibility may be the issue. But for those who go to places where genuine risks are not acknowledged, tourist safety is jeopardized. Isn't government's first responsibility-to protect its citizens - being overshadowed by political convenience? Or does the larger national interest dictate that health and security threats from friendly nations be treated differently from those from unfriendly ones?

For example, some countries with good records on tourist health and safety like Iran and Libya are nations to which U.S. travel is either forbidden or called "extremely dangerous." Meanwhile, Guatemala— where rapes of students in broad daylight and banditry are frequent— has only a mild U.S. advisory Critics have charged that the U.S. having brokered the Guatemalan civil war truce and being lobbied by investors who have massively increased holdings-did not want to protect tourists as much as the Guatemalan economy. Similar considerations appear to have influenced the "watering down" of advisories about Egypt, one of the three top recipients of U.S. aid, and about Mexico, whose bailout needed tourism for repayment. In general, however, most experts concede that the warnings are generally warranted. Now posted by U.S. Consular Affairs on the Internet as well as available from the State Department, the advisories have a global impact.

Japan has been historically even more protective of its traveling citizens. The national economy of some nations has been hurt by a simple announcement from the Japanese government detailing some health or security threat abroad. Japanese citizens respecting the credibility of the government advisories followed the recommendations immediately. Public sector employees need training in thinking through their responsibility to their profession, to the institutions involved in making health and security advisories, and to the larger public interest. Pressures from superiors and constituents may pull the employee in different directions. Few important issues are clearcut. Here, Albert Hirschman's classic Exit, Voice and Loyalty may be helpful in suggesting options and consequences. Institutionalized channels like the U.S. Department of State's dissent channel, offer opportunity for responsible and confidential debate.

Accidents are another major source of injuries and fatalities for travelers. The July 1999 canyoning deaths of 19 adventurers in the Alps, and the numerous fatalities that have accompanied the commercialization of Mt. Everest treks have raised additional ethical questions. Should there be tighter controls on popular but potentially dangerous activities? If so, how much of the burden of filling in the details of such policy will fall to civil servants?

Inadequate signage is another significant contributor to accidents. The use of international signage that communicates through pictures rather than a specific language is widespread in Europe, Australia, and New Zealand, but more scarce in the United States B where foreign visitors have far more accidents in the U.S. than citizens B and rare in developing countries. The World Travel Organization (WTO) has urged member nations to increase international signage.

The whole literature on bureaucratic discretion details the scope for and the extreme care public employees need to take in making "street level" decisions. Requiring more safety measures to be taken or insisting on more experience from those participating on so-called "adventure tours" is a possible approach, but others may argue that the doctrine of caveat emptor relieves the government of responsibility for their safety. Becoming more proactive on behalf of tourist and non-tourist health and safety, however, is fraught with controversy whether at the local public health office or at the international level. Many people have a visceral distrust of government. Also, there are often legitimate needs to go slow, to build consensus, to protect investments, and to avoid "crying wolf" and thereby destroying citizen confidence.

But, we are in a more litigious political environment in many countries. Thus, even if the population is unenthusiastic about some expenditures for health, safety, and accessibility, that same public may expect government to fulfill its core role of keeping them safe. Public sector training that emphasizes thinking through long and short term considerations, doing contingency planning and generally seeking to put in place cooperative internal and international mechanisms to deal with such crises is vital.

Problems in Educational Tourism

Individual tourism is governed by consumer law and government policies, but public educational institutions have additional ethical issues surrounding their international student services and study abroad programs for their own citizens. Such situations are only beginning to be addressed.

International educational travel is complicated by the fact that the students are typically 18-22 -at the prime time in their lives for risktaking behavior. They may be going to countries with unfamiliar laws and customs. Sexual freedom varies markedly around the world. The prospect of running afoul of drug, drinking, or other laws needs to be addressed as the laws differ greatly in severity.

Because international students often bring financial as well as educational and cultural benefits, universities in many countries are increasingly involved in recruitment of such students. International study opportunities are seen as an important dimension of a student's career. Exchanges, study tours, international internships and community service projects abroad are some ways in which universities structure college credit and travel-sometimes with established procedures and appropriate supervision, sometimes merely with eager faculty and a tour company.

Some recent statistics illustrate the magnitude of the issue. Over the past decade the numbers of Americans studying abroad have doubled, from 48,483 in 1985-86 to 99,448 in 1996-97. Most of that growth has occurred in the 1990s. Such students are only about a fifth of the 480,000 foreign students to the United States, but American interest is mushrooming. From the mid 1980s to the mid 1990s, foreign enrollments in the United States increased by about 40 percent, while American students abroad increased by 105 percent.

American student travel abroad has also become much more diverse. In the mid 1980s nearly 80 percent of all travel was to Europe; by 1996-97 that percentage had dropped to 64 percent. Travel to Latin America had more than doubled and other, predominantly developing nations were increasing their share. In many cases, the geographic diversification has left students exposed to greater risks and their supervisors unprepared for coping with the sheer variety of threats to health and safety.

Economic competition, recruiting, and a genuine belief in the educational value of such opportunities keep educators committed to their expansion. The United States is not the only country dealing with these issues. In Australia, New Zealand, and throughout Europe, the practice of student travel is well ahead of the U.S. pace. In many of these societies, vacations are longer and government policies subsidize the travel of youth and workers. Still, consideration of ethical and legal issues of such travel has been slow to keep pace.

The first key issue is quality control. In many places, there is no litmus test or set of standards for the myriad of existing programs nor set requirements for the faculty leading tours. Is the emphasis on increasing numbers coming at the expense of adequate preparation of those traveling internationally? This may be in terms of language preparation or more basic screening. On what basis are students and faculty refused the right to participate? What are the criteria, the processes, and the responsibilities by which specific individuals are given institutional authorization to lead groups abroad?

Are there any screening requirements in addition to academic criteria that can assess the mental health or emotional maturity of participants? If not, shouldn't there be? Some students and faculty are subject to crippling depression when put in entirely new surroundings even without language and customs barriers.

Are there any screening requirements in addition to academic criteria that can assess the mental health or emotional maturity of participants? If not, shouldn't there be? Some students and faculty are subject to crippling depression when put in entirely new surroundings even without language and customs barriers.

Secondly, this raises the dilemma of privacy versus the institution's need to know. To what extent is obtaining information on a student's or faculty member's mental and physical condition itself an invasion of privacy? What legal information is appropriate?

A third issue has to do with the nature and type of orientation, if any, offered to or required of those going abroad. Are students made aware of the health and safety risks of excess drinking abroad, accidents in unfamiliar settings, the penalties for illicit drugs, restrictions on women and the political situation into which they are going?

Finally, should national or institutional policies acknowledge or explicitly waive responsibility for warning travelers of health and security risks? How can institutions protect themselves, their students and their faculty?

Reasonable accommodations for people with disabilities constitute still another set of ethical issues for government personnel serving outside the country and students seeking an international study or work experience. The United States has gone further than any other nation in providing access to transport, accommodations, and attractions for people with disabilities thanks to the Americans with Disabilities Act. Yet issues of fairness remain. Should special needs students have separate but comparable opportunities or is there a value for people with disabilities and able-bodied people to travel together? Should all trips enjoying official government or university sponsorship be accessible for people with disabilities even if it means that groups cannot go some places or that additional costs would be involved? Should individuals with disabilities be subsidized in order to equalize their opportunities? Or should a more utilitarian approach be adopted arguing for the greatest good for the greatest number? Should students with disabilities pay the differential in travel costs for sign language, braille information, wheelchair accessible sites, or personal attendants?

Currently there is no clear legal standard for making such decisions. Rather individual universities are making decisions based on their own resources and notions of fairness. Two private universities, for example, responded to this issue in quite different ways. When Kalen Feeney, a deaf student, applied to go to London on one of Willamette University's study abroad programs, the university paid for an interpreter, even though that meant over $10,000 in additional university costs. The College of St. Scholastica opted not to provide a sign language interpreter for one of its students wanting to go to Ireland. These and other cases raise several ethical questions of fairness and distributive justice, of utilitarian or Rawlsian notions of decisionmaking. There is also the question of whether administrators should pursue defensive or proactive strategies with respect to accessibility issues. While U.S. courts have not applied domestic ADA requirements to university study abroad programs, coordinators of the program must still wrestle with their responsibilities to make such experiences available to all students. In other countries, the dialogue about these issues has scarcely begun. And then there's the question of gender and sexual orientation. Should universities only establish international exchanges with countries having comparable non-discrimination policies? Or, does that defeat the advantage of study and research abroad which is to experience countries with different values? These issues by no means exhaust the travel-related ethical problems with which public sector personnel must grapple. However, they suggest the breadth of concerns with respect to health, safety, and accessibility that must be confronted.

Initiatives to Fight against Ethical Issues

There is an unusual but enormous threat to public health, security, and accessibility from the huge growth and multiple facets of travel and tourism. Deregulation, privatization, heightened competition for tourists of all types, and a sharp increase in the proclivity and ability to travel combine to make tourism and other forms of travel a stew of ethical problems for the public administrator.

These can be challenging for public sector training to address. Still, there are mechanisms that could potentially deal with these issues. At the most general level, there are Codes of Ethics. The International Personnel Management Association (IPMA), the American Society for Public Administration (ASPA), and the International City/County Management Association (ICMA) are but a few of the professional societies that address in their Codes of Ethics broad guidance that could be applicable to travel and tourism. These Codes of Ethics include general advice on avoiding conflicts of interest, abusing the public trust, and serving the public fairly and compassionately. However, nowhere is the public sector employee charged with responsibility for recognizing and coping with the complexity of issues that surround tourism and the public interest. Too often, it is simply assumed that more tourism is desirable. If, as we have seen, health, safety and accessibility issues are neglected, travel and tourism may threaten the public interest.

The tourism industry has begun to recognize this. Efforts are underway to develop a Global Code of Ethics for the industry. However, it is not clear whether the tourism sector will recognize that the various components of the world's largest industry must be partners with the public sector in not only creating sustainable tourism, but also in maintaining healthy, safe, and accessible destinations.

Several codes of ethics for travelers have been developed, which are excellent in encouraging responsible behavior by tourists. These evidence concern for host peoples' customs, feelings, and economic condition, but they do not address health, security, and accessibility issues. Nor are there, to our knowledge, any codes by host destinations except perhaps in the area of consumer protection in terms of tours, accommodations, and purchases.

The World Health Organization's performance remains a critical gap in developing a coordinated strategy. It was founded at a time of very little international travel, much smaller global populations, and when many infectious diseases now plaguing the planet were unknown. Since 1976, over thirty new infectious diseases have been identified, but out-of-date monitoring and disclosure mechanisms at WHO failed to alert the member nations.

Approaching its half century, these challenges of organizational identity and continued relevance confront the World Health Organization. However, the key issue is not how WHO will respond but whether it will respond at all. The existing leadership of WHO has adopted a fortress mentality, fighting bitterly to sustain the status quo and meanwhile allowing good will and opportunities for revitalisation to slip away. The Organization is demonstrably off-course-untrue to itself and consequently suffering from both a myriad of internal ailments and a loss of the intellectual coherence that is essential for global health leadership.

In 1999 new guidelines and information were released by WHO amidst signs that a health crisis looms, but it remains to be seen if member nations will act to avert a disaster. They failed to do so with the AIDS epidemic, which afforded much more time for coordinated responses than Ebola, Rift Fever, the Marburg Virus, and viral pneumonia Will. These emerging health threats are symptomatic of many of the new challenges raised by increased globalization, and they require comprehensive, sustained policy responses.

A network of this sort need not be built entirely from scratch. For example, the WHO has recently established a global surveillance network, called WHONET, linking microbiology labs around the world to a central database.

The U.S. Centers for Disease Control and health counterparts throughout the world provide immense quantities Of data, but each nation processes information through the prism of its own national interest. The traveling public and the host society are not necessarily protected in the process, since few nations have the political will to warn non-citizens and thereby risk decreasing tourism. Moreover, in a federal system like the United States, linkages from the Centers for Disease

Control down to local public health offices may be routine, but incomplete and underutilized. Enormous outbreaks of E. coli infections in the United States in the summer of 1999 were possible because of gaps between the Environmental Protection Agency and local jurisdictions in monitoring the water supply. In one case, more than a thousand people were sickened and several died from contaminated water at a state fair. Because the fair was not a permanent attraction, regulations did not require the kind of scrutiny that was obviously necessary.

In developing nations, information, monitoring, and sanctions are even more erratic and problematic, because the public sector lacks the capacity to implement policies even if a consensus existed on what needed to be done. Such countries are particularly reluctant to work with bodies such as the WHO or international carriers by attempting to document outbreaks of infectious disease. Why raise fears the nation cannot address and at the same time discourage the tourism so vital for foreign exchange?

The World Bank has once more signaled an intention to get back into making loans for tourism development, largely halted in the 1980s. It will be important to see that new development provides a healthier and more accessible infrastructure for the host societies and not merely the tourism enclaves for the affluent outsider that too often characterized past World Bank tourism aid.

In the foreseeable future, the Internet and the private sector will provide the vast bulk of information about travel and tourism, albeit without any quality control for accuracy There are, however, more encouraging consequences of the cyber-revolution. A large global e-mail network, The Program to Monitor Emerging Diseases (PROMED), was initiated in 1993 by doctors who on their own are monitoring health conditions within their borders. Today, there are more than 10,000 subscribers in 130 countries. There are also modest signs that protecting their citizens against the traveling public or lapses in security abroad is becoming an increased responsibility of governments.

Global Code of Ethics for Tourism

Adopted by resolution A/RES/406(XIII) at the thirteenth WTO General Assembly (Santiago, Chile, 27 September - 1 October 1999).

Preamble

We, Members of the World Tourism Organization (WTO), representatives of the world tourism industry, delegates of States, territories, enterprises, institutions and bodies that are gathered for the General Assembly at Santiago, Chile on this first day of October 1999,

Reasserting the aims set out in Article 3 of the Statutes of the World Tourism Organization, and aware of the "decisive and central" role of this Organization, as recognized by the General Assembly of the United Nations, in promoting and developing tourism with a view to contributing to economic development, international understanding, peace, prosperity and universal respect for, and observance of, human rights and fundamental freedoms for all without distinction as to race, sex, language or religion,

Firmly believing that, through the direct, spontaneous and non-mediatized contacts it engenders between men and women of different cultures and lifestyles, tourism represents a vital force for peace and a factor of friendship and understanding among the peoples of the world,

In keeping with the rationale of reconciling environmental protection, economic development and the fight against poverty in a sustainable manner, as formulated by the United Nations in 1992 at the "Earth Summit" of Rio de Janeiro and expressed in Agenda 21, adopted on that occasion,

Taking into account the swift and continued growth, both past and foreseeable, of the tourism activity, whether for leisure, business, culture, religious or health purposes, and its powerful effects, both positive and negative, on the environment, the economy and the society of both generating and receiving countries, on local communities and indigenous peoples, as well as on international relations and trade,

Aiming to promote responsible, sustainable and universally accessible tourism in the framework of the right of all persons to use their free time for leisure pursuits or travel with respect for the choices of society of all peoples,

But convinced that the world tourism industry as a whole has much to gain by operating in an environment that favours the market economy, private enterprise and free trade and that serves to optimize its beneficial effects on the creation of wealth and employment,

Also firmly convinced that, provided a number of principles and a certain number of rules are observed, responsible and sustainable tourism is by no means incompatible with the growing liberalization of the conditions governing trade in services and under whose aegis the enterprises of this sector operate and that it is possible to reconcile in this sector economy and ecology, environment and development, openness to international trade and protection of social and cultural identities,

Considering that, with such an approach, all the stakeholders in tourism development - national, regional and local administrations, enterprises, business associations, workers in the sector, non-governmental organizations and bodies of all kinds belonging to the tourism industry, as well as host communities, the media and the tourists themselves, have different albeit interdependent responsibilities in the individual and societal development of tourism and that the formulation of their individual rights and duties will contribute to meeting this aim,

Committed, in keeping with the aims pursued by the World Tourism Organization itself since adopting resolution 364(XII) at its General Assembly of 1997 (Istanbul), to promote a genuine partnership between the public and private stakeholders in tourism development, and wishing to see a partnership and cooperation of the same kind extend, in an open and balanced way, to the relations between generating and receiving countries and their respective tourism industries,

Following up on the Manila Declarations of 1980 on World Tourism and of 1997 on the Social Impact of Tourism, as well as on the Tourism Bill of Rights and the Tourist Code adopted at Sofia in 1985 under the aegis of WTO,

But believing that these instruments should be complemented by a set of interdependent principles for their interpretation and application on which the stakeholders in tourism development should model their conduct at the dawn of the twenty-first century,

Using, for the purposes of this instrument, the definitions and classifications applicable to travel, and especially the concepts of "visitor", "tourist" and "tourism", as adopted by the Ottawa International Conference, held from 24 to 28 June 1991 and approved, in 1993, by the United Nations Statistical Commission at its twentyseventh session,

Referring in particular to the following instruments:

— Universal Declaration of Human Rights of 10 December 1948;

— International Covenant on Economic, Social and Cultural Rights of 16 December 1966; International Covenant on Civil and Political Rights of 16 December 1966;

— Warsaw Convention on Air Transport of 12 October 1929;

— Chicago Convention on International Civil Aviation of 7 December 1944, and the Tokyo, The Hague and Montreal Conventions in relation thereto;

— Convention on Customs Facilities for Tourism of 4 July 1954 and related Protocol;

— Convention concerning the Protection of the World Cultural and Natural Heritage of 23 November 1972;

— Manila Declaration on World Tourism of 10 October 1980;

— Resolution of the Sixth General Assembly of WTO (Sofia) adopting the Tourism Bill of Rights and Tourist Code of 26 September 1985;

— Convention on the Rights of the Child of 20 November 1989;

— Resolution of the Ninth General Assembly of WTO (Buenos Aires) concerning in particular travel facilitation and the safety and security of tourists of 4 October 1991;

— Rio Declaration on the Environment and Development of 13 June 1992;

— General Agreement on Trade in Services of 15 April 1994;

— Convention on Biodiversity of 6 January 1995;

— Resolution of the Eleventh General Assembly of WTO (Cairo) on the prevention of organized sex tourism of 22 October 1995;

— Stockholm Declaration of 28 August 1996 against the Commercial Sexual Exploitation of Children;Manila Declaration on the Social Impact of Tourism of 22 May 1997;

— Conventions and recommendations adopted by the International Labour Organization in the area of collective conventions, prohibition of forced labour and child labour, defence of the rights of indigenous peoples, and equal treatment and non-discrimination in the work place;

affirm the right to tourism and the freedom of tourist movements,

state our wish to promote an equitable, responsible and sustainable world tourism order, whose benefits will be shared by all sectors of society in the context of an open and liberalized international economy, and

solemnly adopt to these ends the principles of the Global Code of Ethics for Tourism.

Article 1. Tourism's contribution to mutual understanding and respect between peoples and societies

1. The understanding and promotion of the ethical values common to humanity, with an attitude of tolerance and respect for the diversity of religious, philosophical and moral beliefs, are both the foundation and the consequence of responsible tourism; stakeholders in tourism development and tourists themselves should observe the social and cultural traditions and practices

of all peoples, including those of minorities and indigenous peoples and to recognize their worth;

2. Tourism activities should be conducted in harmony with the attributes and traditions of the host regions and countries and in respect for their laws, practices and customs;

3. The host communities, on the one hand, and local professionals, on the other, should acquaint themselves with and respect the tourists who visit them and find out about their lifestyles, tastes and expectations; the education and training imparted to professionals contribute to a hospitable welcome;

4. It is the task of the public authorities to provide protection for tourists and visitors and their belongings; they must pay particular attention to the safety of foreign tourists owing to the particular vulnerability they may have; they should facilitate the introduction of specific means of information, prevention, security, insurance and assistance consistent with their needs; any attacks, assaults, kidnappings or threats against tourists or workers in the tourism industry, as well as the wilful destruction of tourism facilities or of elements of cultural or natural heritage should be severely condemned and punished in accordance with their respective national laws;

5. When travelling, tourists and visitors should not commit any criminal act or any act considered criminal by the laws of the country visited and abstain from any conduct felt to be offensive or injurious by the local populations, or likely to damage the local environment; they should refrain from all trafficking in illicit drugs, arms, antiques, protected species and products and substances that are dangerous or prohibited by national regulations;

6. Tourists and visitors have the responsibility to acquaint themselves, even before their departure, with the characteristics of the countries they are preparing to visit; they must be aware of the health and security risks inherent in any travel outside their usual environment and behave in such a way as to minimize those risks;

Article 2. Tourism as a vehicle for individual and collective fulfilment

1. Tourism, the activity most frequently associated with rest and relaxation, sport and access to culture and nature, should be planned and practised as a privileged means of individual and collective fulfilment; when practised with a sufficiently open mind, it is an irreplaceable factor of self-education, mutual tolerance and for learning about the legitimate differences between peoples and cultures and their diversity;
2. Tourism activities should respect the equality of men and women; they should promote human rights and, more particularly, the individual rights of the most vulnerable groups, notably children, the elderly, the handicapped, ethnic minorities and indigenous peoples;
3. The exploitation of human beings in any form, particularly sexual, especially when applied to children, conflicts with the fundamental aims of tourism and is the negation of tourism; as such, in accordance with international law, it should be energetically combatted with the cooperation of all the States concerned and penalized without concession by the national legislation of both the countries visited and the countries of the perpetrators of these acts, even when they are carried out abroad;

4. Travel for purposes of religion, health, education and cultural or linguistic exchanges are particularly beneficial forms of tourism, which deserve encouragement;

5. The introduction into curricula of education about the value of tourist exchanges, their economic, social and cultural benefits, and also their risks, should be encouraged;

Article 3. Tourism, a factor of sustainable development

1. All the stakeholders in tourism development should safeguard the natural environment with a view to achieving sound, continuous and sustainable economic growth geared to satisfying equitably the needs and aspirations of present and future generations;

2. All forms of tourism development that are conducive to saving rare and precious resources, in particular water and energy, as well as avoiding so far as possible waste production, should be given priority and encouraged by national, regional and local public authorities;

3. The staggering in time and space of tourist and visitor flows, particularly those resulting from paid leave and school holidays, and a more even distribution of holidays should be sought so as to reduce the pressure of tourism activity on the environment and enhance its beneficial impact on the tourism industry and the local economy;

4. Tourism infrastructure should be designed and tourism activities programmed in such a way as to protect the natural heritage composed of ecosystems and biodiversity and to preserve endangered species of wildlife; the stakeholders in tourism development, and especially professionals, should agree to the

imposition of limitations or constraints on their activities when these are exercised in particularly sensitive areas: desert, polar or high mountain regions, coastal areas, tropical forests or wetlands, propitious to the creation of nature reserves or protected areas;

5. Nature tourism and ecotourism are recognized as being particularly conducive to enriching and enhancing the standing of tourism, provided they respect the natural heritage and local populations and are in keeping with the carrying capacity of the sites;

Article 4. Tourism, a user of the cultural heritage of mankind and a contributor to its enhancement

1. Tourism resources belong to the common heritage of mankind; the communities in whose territories they are situated have particular rights and obligations to them;
2. Tourism policies and activities should be conducted with respect for the artistic, archaeological and cultural heritage, which they should protect and pass on to future generations; particular care should be devoted to preserving and upgrading monuments, shrines and museums as well as archaeological and historic sites which must be widely open to tourist visits; encouragement should be given to public access to privately-owned cultural property and monuments, with respect for the rights of their owners, as well as to religious buildings, without prejudice to normal needs of worship;
3. Financial resources derived from visits to cultural sites and monuments should, at least in part, be used for the upkeep, safeguard, development and embellishment of this heritage;
4. Tourism activity should be planned in such a way as to allow traditional cultural products, crafts and

folklore to survive and flourish, rather than causing them to degenerate and become standardized ;

Article 5. Tourism, a beneficial activity for host countries and communities

1. Local populations should be associated with tourism activities and h a re equitably in the economic, social and cultural benefits they generate, and particularly in the reation of direct and indirect jobs resulting from them;
2. Tourism policies should be applied in such a way as to help to raise the standard of living of the populations of the regions visited and meet their needs; the planning and architectural approach to and operation of tourism resorts and accommodation should aim to integrate them, to the extent possible, in the local economic and social fabric; where skills are equal, priority should be given to local manpower;
3. Special attention should be paid to the specific problems of coastal areas and island territories and to vulnerable rural or mountain regions, for which tourism often re p resents a rare opportunity for development in the face of the decline of traditional economic activities;
4. Tourism professionals, particularly investors, governed by the regulations laid down by the public authorities, should carry out studies of the impact of their development projects on the environment and natural surroundings; they should also deliver, with the greatest transparency and objectivity, information on their future programmes and their foreseeable repercussions and foster dialogue on their contents with the populations concerned;

Article 6. Obligations of stakeholders in tourism development

1. Tourism professionals have an obligation to provide tourists with objective and honest information on their places of destination and on the conditions of travel, hospitality and stays; they should ensure that the contractual clauses proposed to their customers are readily understandable as to the nature, price and quality of the services they commit themselves to providing and the financial compensation payable by them in the event of a unilateral breach of contract on their part;
2. Tourism professionals, insofar as it depends on them, should show concern, in cooperation with the public authorities, for the security and safety, accident prevention, health protection and food safety of those who seek their services; likewise, they should ensure the existence of suitable systems of insurance and assistance; they should accept the reporting obligations prescribed by national regulations and pay fair compensation in the event of failure to observe their contractual obligations;
3. Tourism professionals, so far as this depends on them, should contribute to the cultural and spiritual fulfilment of tourists and allow them, during their travels, to practise their religions;
4. The public authorities of the generating States and the host countries, in cooperation with the professionals concerned and their associations, should ensure that the necessary mechanisms are in place for the repatriation of tourists in the event of the bankruptcy of the enterprise that organized their travel;
5. Governments have the right - and the duty - especially in a crisis, to inform their nationals of the difficult

circumstances, or even the dangers they may encounter during their travels abroad; it is their responsibility however to issue such information without prejudicing in an unjustified or exaggerated manner the tourism industry of the host countries and the interests of their own operators; the contents of travel advisories should therefore be discussed beforehand with the authorities of the host countries and the professionals concerned; recommendations formulated should be strictly proportionate to the gravity of the situations encountered and confined to the geographical areas where the insecurity has arisen; such advisories should be qualified or cancelled as soon as a return to normality permits;

6. The press, and particularly the specialized travel press and the other media, including modern means of electronic communication, should issue honest and balanced information on events and situations that could influence the flow of tourists; they should also provide accurate and reliable information to the consumers of tourism services; the new communication and electronic commerce technologies should also be developed and used for this purpose; as is the case for the media, they should not in any way promote sex tourism;

Article 7. Right to tourism

1. The prospect of direct and personal access to the discovery and enjoyment of the planet's resources constitutes a right equally open to all the world's inhabitants; the increasingly extensive participation in national and international tourism should be regarded as one of the best possible expressions of the sustained growth of free time, and obstacles should not be placed in its way;

2. The universal right to tourism must be regarded as the corollary of the right to rest and leisure, including reasonable limitation of working hours and periodic holidays with pay, guaranteed by Article 24 of the Universal Declaration of Human Rights and Article 7.d of the International Covenant on Economic, Social and Cultural Rights;
3. Social tourism, and in particular associative tourism, which facilitates widespread access to leisure, travel and holidays, should be developed with the support of the public authorities;
4. Family, youth, student and senior tourism and tourism for people with disabilities, should be encouraged and facilitated;

Article 8. Liberty of tourist movements

1. Tourists and visitors should benefit, in compliance with international law and national legislation, from the liberty to move within their countries and from one State to another, in accordance with Article 13 of the Universal Declaration of Human Rights; they should have access to places of transit and stay and to tourism and cultural sites without being subject to excessive formalities or discrimination;
2. Tourists and visitors should have access to all available forms of communication, internal or external; they should benefit from prompt and easy access to local administrative, legal and health services; they should be free to contact the consular representatives of their countries of origin in compliance with the diplomatic conventions in force;
3. Tourists and visitors should benefit from the same rights as the citizens of the country visited concerning the confidentiality of the personal data and information

concerning them, especially when these are stored electronically;

4. Administrative procedures relating to border crossings whether they fall within the competence of States or result from international agreements, such as visas or health and customs formalities, should be adapted, so far as possible, so as to facilitate to the maximum freedom of travel and widespread access to international tourism; agreements between groups of countries to harmonize and simplify these procedures should be encouraged; specific taxes and levies penalizing the tourism industry and undermining its competitiveness should be gradually phased out or corrected;

5. So far as the economic situation of the countries from which they come permits, travellers should have access to allowances of convertible currencies needed for their travels;

Article 9. Rights of the workers and entrepreneurs in the tourism industry

1. The fundamental rights of salaried and self-employed workers in the tourism industry and related activities, should be guaranteed under the supervision of the national and local administrations, both of their States of origin and of the host countries with particular care, given the specific constraints linked in particular to the seasonality of their activity, the global dimension of their industry and the flexibility often required of them by the nature of their work;

2. Salaried and self-employed workers in the tourism industry and related activities have the right and the duty to acquire appropriate initial and continuous training; they should be given adequate social

protection; job insecurity should be limmited so far as possible; and a specific status, with particular regard to their social welfare, should be offered to seasonal workers in the sector;

3. Any natural or legal person, provided he, she or it has the necessary abilities and skills, should be entitled to develop a professional activity in the field of tourism under existing national laws; entrepreneurs and investors especially in the area of small and medium-sized enterprises - should be entitled to free access to the tourism sector with a minimum of legal or administrative restrictions;

4. Exchanges of experience offered to executives and workers, whether salaried or not, from different countries, contributes to foster the development of the world tourism industry; these movements should be facilitated so far as possible in compliance with the applicable national laws and international conventions;

5. As an irreplaceable factor of solidarity in the development and dynamic growth of international exchanges, multinational enterprises of the tourism industry should not exploit the dominant positions they sometimes occupy; they should avoid becoming the vehicles of cultural and social models artificially imposed on the host communities; in exchange for their freedom to invest and trade which should be fully recognized, they should involve themselves in local development, avoiding, by the excessive repatriation of their profits or their induced imports, a reduction of their contribution to the economies in which they are established;

6. Partnership and the establishment of balanced relations between enterprises of generating and receiving countries contribute to the sustainable

development of tourism and an equitable distribution of the benefits of its growth;

Article 10. Implementation of the principles of the Global Code of Ethics for Tourism

1. The public and private stakeholders in tourism development should cooperate in the implementation of these principles and monitor their effective application;
2. The stakeholders in tourism development should recognize the role of international institutions, among which the World Tourism Organization ranks first, and non-governmental organizations with competence in the field of tourism promotion and development, the protection of human rights, the environment or health, with due respect for the general principles of international law;
3. The same stakeholders should demonstrate their intention to refer any disputes concerning the application or interpretation of the Global Code of Ethics for Tourism for conciliation to an impartial third body known as the World Committee on Tourism Ethics.

7

Role of Local Authorities in Sustainable Tourism

Tourism is recognised as being one of the world's main economic activities. In 2000 there were almost 700 million international arrivals, and it is estimated that domestic tourism accounts for ten times more trips than international travel. Tourism demand was seriously affected by the terrorist attacks in 2001, but appeared to have largely recovered by the summer of 2002. The World Tourism Organisation (WTO) predicts that international tourism will continue to grow by 4 to 4.5% annually over the coming years, with levels of domestic tourism also set to increase.

Tourism has a major impact on local communities in tourist destinations. It can be a significant source of income and employment for local people. It can also pose a threat to an area's social fabric and its natural and cultural heritage, upon which it ultimately depends, but if it is well planned and managed it can be a force for their conservation. These stakes have led to a recognition of the tourism sector's need to incorporate the principles of sustainable development contained in Agenda 21, which was adopted at the Earth Summit in 1992. At an international level, the tourism industry has taken certain initiatives towards this, and guidelines are now available that are relevant at all levels of government.Now there is a need to focus on local action, since "the true proof of 'sustainable tourism' will be the sustainable development of local communities that serve as tourist destinations".

According to the WTO, "Sustainable tourism development meets the needs of present tourists and host regions while protecting and enhancing opportunities for the future." The development of sustainable tourism meets the following requirements:

— Tourist resources - natural, historical, cultural and others - are preserved in a way that allows them to be used in the future, whilst benefiting today's society;

— The planning and management of tourist development are conducted in a way that avoids triggering serious ecological or socio-cultural problems in the region concerned;

— The overall quality of the environment in the tourist region is preserved and, if necessary, improved;

— The level of tourist satisfaction should be maintained to ensure that destinations continue to be attractive and retain their commercial potential; and

— Tourism should largely benefit all members of society.

Traditionally, tourism development has depended on initiatives taken by the private sector. In many countries local authorities have not been closely involved in tourism and have little experience of its planning, development and management.

In recent years this has been changing, and the key role of local authorities is now recognised. This is due to:

— The complexity of the tourism sector, where it is the consumer who is brought to the product and not the other way round, as happens with most other goods and services.

— Increasing awareness that tourists select and respond to destinations, not just individual products. The visitor experience is made up of a complex range of elements including expectations, transport, information, accommodation, attractions, activities, local infrastructure, natural environments, cultural heritage, a welcoming host population, security and other services.

— The disparate nature of the private sector in tourism, much of which comprises small and micro enterprises.

— Acceptance that, in the interests of sustainability, public authorities need to be involved in regulating tourist development in destinations, and not simply leaving it up to the laws of the market.

— The trend towards administrative decentralisation underway in many countries, which increases the ability of local authorities to intervene.

Local authorities have an important role in economic development, including tourism development. They are often the best placed organisations for establishing a sustainable approach to tourism in destinations, setting a strategy and balancing the interests of tourism enterprises, tourists and local residents. Their ability to manage tourism sustainably is related to:

— Their democratic legitimacy;

— Their relative permanence and ability to take a long term view; and

— Their responsibility for a range of functions that can influence tourism development, including spatial planning, development control, environmental management and community services.

The Local Agenda 21 approach

Chapter 28 of Agenda 21 binds local authorities to implementing at a local level the commitments made towards sustainable development by the international community.

A Local Agenda 21 is an approach through which a local community defines a sustainable development strategy and an action programme to be implemented. The approach is usually initiated by the local authority, which provides leadership for the process. Its success hinges on close cooperation between the population, NGOs, private enterprises and other local interests.

The process normally involves five steps:

1. Setting up a Local Agenda 21 Forum and/or working groups;
2. Discussion and analysis of the main local issues;
3. Identification of goals and ideas for action for the sustainable development of the local area;
4. Integration of these goals and ideas into a Local Agenda 21 action plan that is adopted by the local authority and others;
5. Implementation of the action plan, with the involvement of all relevant players.

There is no prescription for what issues and activities the process should address, as all places are different and the principle is to enable partners in each location to identify their own priorities. However, in accordance with Agenda 21, the process should focus on economic, social and environmental sustainability.

The International Council on Local Environmental Initiatives (ICLEI) estimates that more than three and a half thousand local communities worldwide are now establishing or implementing Local Agendas 21. Over the coming years their number should continue to rise, thanks to inter-community networking, international information campaigns and the circulation of training guides and other materials.

Agenda 21. Chapter 28.
Local Authorities' Initiatives in Support of Agenda 21.

Prpgramme Area

Basis for action

28.1. Because so many of the problems and solutions being addressed by Agenda 21 have their roots in local activities, the participation and cooperation of local authorities will be a determining factor in fulfilling its objectives. Local authorities construct, operate and maintain economic, social and environmental infrastructure, oversee planning processes, establish local environmental policies and regulations, and assist in implementing national and subnational environmental policies. As the level of governance closest to the people, they play a vital role in educating, mobilizing and responding to the public to promote sustainable development.

Objectives

28.2. The following objectives are proposed for this programme area:

(a) By 1996, most local authorities in each country should have undertaken a consultative process with their populations and achieved a consensus on "a local Agenda 21" for the community;

(b) By 1993, the international community should have initiated a consultative process aimed at increasing cooperation between local authorities;

(c) By 1994, representatives of associations of cities and other local authorities should have increased levels of cooperation and coordination with the goal of enhancing the exchange of information and experience among local authorities;

(d) All local authorities in each country should be encouraged to implement and monitor programmes which aim at ensuring that women and youth are represented in decision-making, planning and implementation processes.

Activities

28.3. Each local authority should enter into a dialogue with its citizens, local organizations and private enterprises and adopt "a local Agenda 21". Through consultation and consensus-building, local authorities would learn from citizens and from local, civic, community, business and industrial organizations and acquire the information needed for formulating the best strategies.

The process of consultation would increase household awareness of sustainable development issues. Local authority programmes, policies, laws and regulations to achieve Agenda 21 objectives would be assessed and modified, based on local programmes adopted. Strategies could also be used in supporting proposals for local, national, regional and international funding.

28.4. Partnerships should be fostered among relevant organs and organizations such as UNDP, the United Nations Centre for Human Settlements (Habitat) and UNEP, the World Bank, regional banks, the International Union of Local Authorities, the World Association of the Major Metropolises, Summit of Great Cities of the World, the United Towns Organization and other relevant partners, with a view to mobilizing increased international support for local authority programmes. An important goal would be to support, extend and improve existing institutions working in the field of local authority capacity-building and local environment management. For this purpose:

(a) Habitat and other relevant organs and organizations of the United Nations system are called upon to strengthen services in collecting information on strategies of local authorities, in particular for those that need international support;

(b) Periodic consultations involving both international partners and developing countries could review strategies and consider how such international support could best be mobilized. Such a sectoral consultation would complement concurrent country-focused consultations, such as those taking place in consultative groups and round tables.

28.5. Representatives of associations of local authorities are encouraged to establish processes to increase the exchange of information, experience and mutual technical assistance among local authorities.

Means of implementation

(a) Financing and cost evaluation

28.6. It is recommended that all parties reassess funding needs in this area. The UNCED Secretariat has estimated the average total annual cost (1993-2000) for strengthening international secretariat services for implementing the activities in this chapter to be about $1 million on grant or concessional terms. These are indicative and order of magnitude estimates only and have not been reviewed by governments.

(b) Human resource development and capacity-building 28.7. This programme should facilitate the capacity-building and training activities already contained in other chapters of Agenda 21.

Incidence of Local Agenda 21s for tourism

In partnership with the International Council for Local Environmental Initiatives (ICLEI) UNEP conducted a study to looks at how tourism has been taken into account in local Agendas 21, as drawn up and implemented by local authorities. It found that as local authorities face the impacts of tourism development, the Agenda 21 planning framework is useful to define strategic goals for all stakeholders, and to effectively use tourism to achieve a community's main goals. There was no precise information on the extent to which Local Agenda 21 processes have been applied to tourism at a destination level. In this regard, a search for case studies gives some insight about this.The search was for communities that had:

— A global approach to sustainable development, demonstrated by introducing a Local Agenda 21;

— A comprehensive strategy for sustainable tourism, within or linked to the Local Agenda 21, and not merely some individual initiatives;

— Strong leadership by the local authority and a participatory approach.

Examples were found by questioning tourism and municipal bodies and international networks, as well as through the Internet. The search identified a handful of relevant cases where a truly comprehensive and strategic approach to tourism had been taken that related to Local Agenda 21. The search also found a large number of very interesting local initiatives on sustainable or eco-tourism under the aegis of communities or NGOs, but these were one-off initiatives and not part of an overall strategy. Three types of destination showed up most strongly as having tourism strategies linked to Local Agenda 21:

— *Islands*. On some islands tourism dominates the economy and may even be the sole source of income and employment. Islands are often environmentally vulnerable, facing problems of resource supply and management (such as drinking water and pollution control) and a concentration of tourism in a limited space. An imbalance in the number of tourists and permanent residents may create tension.

— *Historic towns receiving relatively high tourist numbers*. The LA21s conducted by these towns were often found to cover all aspects of sustainable development, with the relative attention given to tourism varying from place to place.

— *Established tourist resorts*. Most of these were in coastal areas. In many resorts the importance of sound tourism destination management is increasingly recognised by the local authority, often because of past problems with uncontrolled or harmful development.

There may be various explanations for the fact that only a handful of cases were identified:

— A lack of involvement in sustainability issues by tourist destinations. Some places may be reaping the economic benefits of tourism development without seeing the need to make this a more sustainable process. Longterm problems arising from traffic, pollution, price rises, etc. may not be immediately apparent to local residents.

— The difficulty in identifying communities that are taking a strategic approach to tourism. Initiatives taken by the private sector may be more visible than local authority strategies.

— The number of sustainable tourism strategies that are not nominally related to Local Agenda 21. Not everyone is aware of LA21. Several communities contacted did not recognise the term or know what it meant. This varies between countries, partly due to the level of publicity given to the process.

The last of these three points is particularly important. It must be accepted that interesting and effective national, regional or local tourism strategies are also being conducted, drawing on the principles of sustainability and using a participatory approach, but using other names for the process and with no explicit reference to Local Agenda 21. The concern should be for achieving e ffective results, not about the adherence to terminology. All of this goes to show how important it is to identify local communities with sustainable tourism strategies, in order to facilitate the exchange of experience and to enhance know-how.

Selection of Case Studies

The selection of case studies reflected the diversity of types of destination and tourism-related issues encountered: mature and emerging destinations, urban, seaside and rural tourism, and regions under both high and more moderate tourist pressure.

The following were chosen:

— *Bournemouth (UK)* has 151,000 inhabitants. An established and aff l u e n t resort in the South of England, it receives some 1.5 million tourists each year, plus 4.5 million day-trippers. Bournemouth is known as a holiday destination and as a centre for conference and business tourism. In 1995, Bournemouth adopted a "Declaration of Commitment" for a LA21. The Bournemouth Community Plan 2000-2005, signed by 100 partners, was officially recognised as the LA21 strategy in 2002.

— *Calvià (Balearic Islands, Spain)* is a community in the South of Majorca. It has a population of around, 42,000 and 120,000 beds. It is one of the Mediterranean's leading tourist resorts. It experienced the tourism boom of the sixties, followed by a crisis in the late eighties. Following two years of study and discussion, Calvià approved an ambitious LA21 strategy.

— *Winchester (UK)* has 35,000 inhabitants in the city itself (111,700 in the District). The former capital of England, it has an outstanding cultural and historical heritage in a well-preserved rural region. Tourism is one of the region's main economic activities. Day trips account for 90 percent of visitors. Since 1997 Winchester has been involved in an LA21 strategy and in an integral quality management approach in the field of tourism.

— *Storstrøm County (Denmark)* covers 24 communities with a total of 260,000 inhabitants. It is an affluent, largely industrial and agricultural region, which is also striving to guide its tourism sector towards sustainabili t y. The County unanimously adopted the LA21 Action Plan in 1997. A l o n g term LA21 strategy is currently being prepared.

— *Marie-Galante (French Caribbean)* is a small island in the French West Indies. It has a population of 12,500. It is an agricultural and rural island that has been left untouched by development. It is striving to develop its as yet very limited tourist activity. The three communities on the island joined forces on their development strategy, and in 1999 adopted a LA21 programme.

Whatever the level of current response, there are a number of reasons why local authorities should consider developing a sustainable tourism strategy within the context of Local Agenda 21. It will:

— Ensure that tourism planning and development address key issues relating to the economic, social, and environmental impact of tourism in the long and short term;

— Place tourism within the overall context of the sustainable development and environmental management of the community;

— Provide a framework for, and give legitimacy to, the participation of a range of stakeholders in tourism and representatives of the local community;

— Raise the profile of tourism and the tourism strategy within the community;

— Strengthen the position of the authority as an organisation that takes sustainable tourism seriously, with national and international support; and

— Help the destination to attract the attention of visitors and tour operators keen to visit or work with sustainable destinations.

Evidence from the case studies, which describe different problems of tourism development and sustainability, shows that the LA 21 approach can be adapted to different situations and have different objectives for tourism. Four typical objectives for LA21 are listed below.

1 . To Meet a Preventive Goal

Bournemouth has long enjoyed a good reputation as far as the quality of its environment is concerned, and its tourist activity is thriving and expanding. The town's LA21 is of a preventive nature, intended to maintain this high quality environment and attractiveness. It seeks the best possible management of the growth of tourist activity to which it aspires. The town has set itself the target of increasing the number of conference visitors and out of season tourism by 5% by 2005. The strategy of the LA21 is to pursue awards that would enable Bournemouth as a whole to be marketed as an "environmental" destination.

2 . *To Address Existing Problems*

Calvià has been the victim of uncontrolled growth of tourism, degradation of the tourist product and a drop in tourist numbers. Its LA21 has a curative aim: to restore the resort and the surrounding landscape, to limit the increase in the number of beds, to demolish unsuitable facilities, to improve the quality of amenities, and to develop appropriate products. The LA21 is a genuine longterm overall strategy for reshaping the destination's approach to tourism development.

3 . *To Strike a Balance between the Needs of Tourists and Residents*

Winchester is an historic town that is exposed to strong tourist pressure. The LA21 approach looks to limit the downside of tourism as experienced by residents (negative environmental effects, congestion, pollution, risk of degradation of sensitive sites and monuments, etc.). These negative effects are further exacerbated by the remarkably high numbers of day-trippers, who generate a cost for the community whilst producing relatively little economic spin-off compared to overnight visitors. Therefore, the aim of the strategy is to encourage longer-stay tourism and to maximise the profits generated by tourist activity.

4 . *To Stimulate Sustainable Development*

Marie-Galante is seeking economic, social and cultural development based on sustainable tourism, which preserves the environment and respects local populations. It is seeking to establish itself as a tourist destination, building upon its strong cultural identity and the quality of its environment. It rejects the mass tourism found in some other parts of the Caribbean, and seeks self-determination. The local Agenda 21 approach is also a cultural project, which aims to open up future prospects for the population. It sets great store by the social and economic dimensions of sustainability.

LA21 can also be used to achieve a combination of these goals, as illustrated by Storstrøm County. These examples clearly show that local communities have very different concerns regarding sustainable tourism, but that the LA21 instrument has proved to be well adapted to their intended aims, no matter how varied they may be. It is applicable to established and emerging destinations, and to those in good condition as well as those with economic or environmental problems. All types of destination potentially face the need to re-think their line of tourism development, and all can benefit from defining a strategy aimed at developing a more sustainable form of tourism.

Managementment Process and Actions

There are three components of a successful strategy and action plan for tourism in the context of Local Agenda 21:

— Establishing effective structures for multi-stakeholder participation, both in setting the direction for tourism in the community and in working together to develop and manage it.

— Identifying a strategy for sustainable tourism within the context of a wider sustainable development strategy that reflects stakeholders views and that allows tourism management to be integrated with other management functions in the destination.

— Identifying and implementing a set of actions, in line with the strategy, that address the economic, social and environmental sustainability of tourism in the area.

For each of these three elements, the experience of the five case studies has been used to inform and illustrate recommendations to local authorities.

Leadership and Partnership Structures

A fundamental requirement of Local Agenda 21 is a bottom-up approach, with the local community closely involved in determining a sustainable future for its area. However such a process needs direction and leadership. Of course, participatory approaches involving both citizens and enterprises are not specific to the tourism sector.

Provide leadership and facilitation through the local authority: Local authorities are usually well placed to provide leadership on sustainable development and management issues, including tourism. To be effective, they must strike the right balance between leadership and facilitation. Local authorities often take the initiative for launching Local Agenda 21 and for tailoring it to suit the local situation. They organise and coordinate the participation of others, and implement the actions for which they are responsible. For example, they may provide the various other players with environmental and business support services, such as information, guidance, training, etc., to encourage and enable them to subscribe to the process.

Some authorities will have the necessary skills, including tourism knowledge, to undertake this function. Others may need to acquire them through recruitment, training, or outside assistance.

Clearly, the structure, responsibilities, strength and resources of local authorities will vary from country to country. In some cases, provincial authorities and local municipalities will need to work together, especially in rural areas where municipalities may be too small to undertake the necessary management functions or to relate to viable tourism destinations.

Involve both the environment and tourism departments: Frequently, the LA21 process in local authorities is led by departments, councillors or officers responsible for environmental issues, as it tends to be better known in this sector. This is an advantage when tackling issues such as pollution control and habitat protection, but can mean that the community's economic and social development are not fully addressed in the process. For successful sustainable tourism planning and development it is essential that departments and staff concerned with economic development and tourism, and who understand markets and enterprise realities, are equally involved.

The starting point may vary between authorities. In Bournemouth, the LA21 is led by the environment team, although the tourism department is very much involved and works in close cooperation with them, as do all the Council services. In Winchester the tourism department put a lot of hard thinking into the right type of tourism for the city and was one of the first of the Council's services to switch over to a sustainable development position. It played a significant role in opening the Council's eyes to sustainability, and the Council then committed itself to producing a global LA21.

Seek a high level of political engagement: The fact that tourism touches so many aspects of society, and cuts across such a wide range of, local authority functions, means that it should be addressed at a high level politically and within the executive. This will help to ensure that it is taken into account within the community's overall policy, with effective coordination between departments. Relating tourism to LA21 can help in this respect.

Ensure that broader LA21 participatory structures involve tourism interests: The Local Agenda 21 process requires the establishment of a stakeholder group. This can range from a round table or forum with a limited-term mandate to a new statutory committee with a long-term mandate. Its purpose is to:

— Create a shared common vision for the future;
— Identify and prioritise key issues;
— Ensure an integrated approach;
— Develop action plans, drawing on diverse experiences and knowledge;
— Mobilise community-wide resources; and
— Increase support for municipal activities.

A stakeholder group might include representatives of local businesses, trade unions, community groups, religious organisations, indigenous communities, or different levels of government, among others.

Within the stakeholder group, it is common practice to establish a set of working groups. These groups might be given responsibility for different stages of the vision and planning process, or be asked to look at specific topics and issues. Tourism should be integrated into this process by ensuring that the sector is represented in the stakeholder group and the working group structure. In some areas, tourism may be such an important issue that it becomes central to the work of the community's stakeholder group, or requires the establishment of a dedicated stakeholder group with further working groups looking at specific aspects of tourism. ships commonly involve individual tourism enterprises or representative organisations such as hotel or camping site associations.

It is important to encourage such bodies to promote an interest in sustainability issues amongst their membership and to reflect this in their policies and programmes of action. Local authorities can do this by encouraging them to involve environmental organisations and community groups, not just tourism industry members.

Consult and inform the wider community: Clearly it is not possible to involve all citizens directly in LA 21 bodies. However, there needs to be a process to enable everyone to be informed and to have their say about the sustainable development of their community, including the level and nature of tourism development. This can be achieved through:

— Holding open meetings in different parts of the community;
— Maintaining a good relationship with local media;
— Establishing dedicated communication media such as newsletters and websites; and
— Undertaking resident surveys.

Encourage initiative from others, not just the local authority: Another aspect of partnership is that all those involved initiatives should be able to take action. In Storstrom the "Sustainable Development around Presto Inlet" project was launched at the initiative of a campsite owner who wanted to bring all actors together for local tourism development. The surrounding municipalities then signed up to the project to develop sustainable tourism for the site.

Engage the customer (tour operators and visitors) in the process: The partnership process should be as inclusive as possible. It is increasingly recognised that progress in achieving a more sustainable approach to tourism will require getting the message across to, and accepted by, the marketplace. Tour operators and visitors themselves should be engaged in the process, both by seeking their views and by influencing their actions. It is important to understand their expectations, level of satisfaction, and reaction to sustainability issues and alternative travel and product options.

It is not easy to engage individual tourists directly in stakeholder groups, but they can be brought into the process through regular visitor surveys and through excellent information for them in the destination. Hosts, such as accommodation operators, play an important role in communicating ideas to visitors and passing feedback from them to destination planners and managers.

It is easier to engage representatives of the market, such as incoming tour operators, as stakeholders in the planning process. The views of international operators should be included as well. It is also very important to engage transport providers, as they can have a significant influence on tourist flows and impacts. LA21s tend to be supply-oriented, the link with demand and the market being a relative weakness. Although market assessment has been an important part of tourism planning in destinations, actual dialogue with visitors and tour operators has tended to be rather limited. To some extent this applies to the case study areas as well. However, some of them, such as Winchester, have developed information-gathering and visitor survey mechanisms.

Sustainable Tourism Srategies and Local Management Tools

One of the main purposes of creating partnership structures, is to prepare a widely accepted strategy for the sustainable development of an area that includes tourism.

Ensure that sustainable tourism is integrated within the overall policies and actions towards sustainable development in the area. The LA21 process involves using the stakeholder group and working groups to identify issues, agree on an overall vision, identify strategic priorities, and establish an action programme. The process requires time and careful consultation. Tourism should be considered alongside all other issues relating to sustainable development. The relative level of priority given to tourism will vary from place to place, depending on factors such as the current importance of tourism to the economy, the area's resources, and the desires and aspirations of the community. This is likely to influence how tourism is treated within the LA 21 strategy.

Some options include:

— Developing a LA21 strategy for the area, of which sustainable tourism is the dominant component, as in Calvià;

— Developing a LA21 strategy that contains some policies and actions for sustainable tourism. This has been the case with Storstrøm and Marie-Galante. In both cases, there are aspects of the whole LA21 strategy that have a bearing on tourism, not just those that are specifically identified as tourism policies or actions. For example, in Marie-Galante, various actions on agriculture and handicrafts involve tourism;

— Creating separate sustainable tourism strategies and LA 21 strategies, but ensuring that they take close account of each other in the way they are formed and implemented. This has been the approach in Bournemouth and Winchester.

Ensure that the strategy for sustainable tourism is based on sound analysis: While the strategy for sustainable tourism should be integrated into the overall sustainable development strategy, and be developed through a participatory processes involving stakeholders, it is also important that it is based on a sound analysis and framework. This should include:

— An assessment of the area's socio-economic and environmental circumstances and needs and of how tourism can relate to these;

— An audit of resources and facilities for tourism (including natural and cultural resources, infrastructure, etc.) and an assessment of their strengths and weaknesses;

— An analysis of existing and potential future markets;

— An assessment of existing and potential problems and opportunities brought by tourism, including the environmental performance of tourism businesses;

— A long term vision of tourism in the destination at some future point;

— A set of strategic objectives;

— A set of measurable targets and indicators;

— An action plan, including an indication of resources and responsible players; and

— An identified process for monitoring and review.

Specifically address the economic, social and environmental impacts of tourism within the strategy

This is a key requirement of LA21. In the past, conventional tourism strategies have tended to concentrate mainly on economic needs and opportunities. The principles of LA 21 planning include:

— "A systemic approach that addresses the underlying causes of social, economic and ecological problems in an integrated way, focussing on the entire systems that are affected, rather than only problem symptoms;

— Ecological limits that are defined by the Earth's carrying capacity and serve as the limits for development;

— Equity and justice that are secured locally through the provision of equal opportunities and human rights ..."In terms of tourism, this suggests that there should be an emphasis on issues such as total volumes of tourism, visitor and traffic management, the siting of development, local community attitudes and decision-making, policies towards local employment, access for all without discrimination, retention of income in the local area, etc.

Place special emphasis on the long term vision: This is another fundamental aspect of the LA21 philosophy. Conventional tourism strategies have often focussed on driving a five-year action plan rather than truly setting a path towards future prosperity and sustainability. Clearly, a long-term vision can be used to guide short- and medium-term actions that may emanate from it.

Make sure the strategy is community-owned and community-driven, but also reflects technical expertise: The partnership structures and processes are essential for a tourism strategy based on LA21 principles. The strategy process should be given enough time to enable full participation by stakeholders in identifying issues and ideas and agreeing on directions and solutions. However, there are also many aspects of tourism planning, such as market analysis or assessment of environmental sensitivity and impact, that require technical expertise that may need to be brought in from outside.

Community-based Issues Analysis is generally advocated for LA21 work. The key to success with this is to link together the use of participant assessment exercises and expert technical assessments. Stakeholders should participate in technical assessments and the findings of these assessments should be provided as final input into the participant assessment process. In this way, the full assessment exercise can be used to educate residents and stakeholders, and technical findings can be used to validate participant observation and knowledge (and vice versa).

Integrate tourism into broader planning and management tools and functions: The recommendations outlined above should ensure that sustainable tourism policies and priorities are reflected in the wider policies of the local authority towards sustainability, and vice versa. However, this synergy should also be carried forward into actual management processes on a day-to-day basis. There are a number of important management tools relating both to tourism and to sustainable development that may be used by local authorities in pursuing sustainable tourism and the requirements of LA21. Those that have emerged from the case studies are described below.

— *Spatial planning.* This is a major tool for organising and controlling development, including building and changes in land use. It is extremely important that sustainable tourism policies be reflected in spatial plans and implemented through rigorous notification and determination procedures. Spatial planning has proved a key tool in Calvià, where the new spatial plan includes the declassification of 1,350 hectares of land previously designated for building, the prohibition of new buildings on rural land and the reduction of maximum population density from 1,708 to 1,491 inhabitants per hectare.

— *Carrying capacity or limits of acceptable change.* L A 21 embraces the principle of identifying limits to growth for planning and management purposes. T h e concept of carrying capacity - the number of visitors that a destination is able to absorb without damage to the environment, community or visitor experience - has been widely debated. It was central to Calvià's approach. Current thinking suggests that it may be misleading to think in terms of specific quantities, but rather to specify clearly the limits to acceptable change and the processes for staying within them.

— *Environmental Management System (EMS).* The individual operations and initiatives carried out by the local authority itself, or supported by it, should comply with sustainability principles. An EMS is an effective tool for ensuring the sustainable management of organisations and improving their environmental performance. EMSs, originally designed for private companies, have now begun to spread to local authorities.Bournemouth has adopted an EMS-style approach (without referring to ISO standard 14001) and Storstrøm County is set to follow suit.

— *Integrated Quality Management (IQM).* This concept, long used by industry, has recently been taken up by tourist destinations. Integrated quality management of tourist destinations is a continuous management process that "should simultaneously take into account and have a favourable impact on the activities of tourism professionals, tourists, the local population and the environment (that is the natural, cultural and man-made assets of the destination)".I t involves setting standards, measuring responses and making improvements. The LA21 process and IQM have many points in common, given that the environment plays a major role in destination quality and IQM covers the destination as a whole. However, the central concern of IQM is market understanding and the quality of the visitor experience, which is only partially true for the LA21 process, if at all. The two processes should be conducted in tandem.

— *Environmental charges*. The possibility and benefit of putting a charge on the tourism industry or tourists, to raise revenue for conservation and destination management, has been looked at and pursued in some destinations. A tax introduced in the Balearic Islands including Calvià in March 2002, averaging 1 euro per night, is expected to raise some 60m euros. It has been controversial, drawing opposition from many private sector interests. Voluntary initiatives have been pursued in the UK and elsewhere, but have raised only small sums.

Set goals, targets, indicators and monitoring procedures: The LA21 process requires that strategies (including the sustainable tourism strategy) contain elements that help to ensure that the vision is translated into reality. These include:

— Setting goals that are attainable but also sufficient to achieve the vision over time. These should be agreed amongst stakeholders through the use of priority-setting exercises;

— Setting targets that relate to the goals, and that are achievable and measurable.

The LA21 process identifies four key components for an effective evaluation:

— Establishing a system for all key stakeholders to report to each other on the actions they have taken.

— Developing valid and measurable indicators to measure the performance of the area as a whole. Destinations will vary in terms of what is practicable.

— Implementing a comprehensive analysis and review on a periodic basis.

— Establishing ways of letting everyone in the community know about progress and performance.

Besides the indicators created for study purposes, a small number of simple indicators should also be developed to allow communication with residents, enterprises and tourists. Everyone in the community should be in a position to assess how much ground has been covered on the long road towards sustainable tourism.

Tourism Issues and Actions Relating to Local Agenda 21

The philosophy behind LA21 is that circumstances in each community will be d i fferent and that priorities and actions should therefore be determined by the communities themselves through the processes outlined above. However, a number of areas for action that are particularly relevant to sustainable tourism and LA21, and that have been highlighted by the case studies, are discussed below. These are actions that seek to promote environmental, social and economic sustainability. Many of them benefit all three, and are mutually reinforcing rather than discrete actions.

Improve environmental planning and management in the destination: Some issues and actions involve the physical development of tourism. This can include:

— *Location and control of new development.* The new strict planning policies towards tourism in Calvià have already been mentioned;

— *Rehabilitation of the built environment.* In Calvià, the community has purchased key sites, and has demolished unsuitable buildings to recreate public open space and a better-quality landscape;

— *Careful design of new development,* such as low-impact yacht harbours in Marie-Galante.

Provision of environmental control measures and relevant local services, such as monitoring and improving air and water quality, litter clearance, provision of waste recycling schemes, etc. are all functions of local authorities that are relevant to the quality of tourism destinations. Beach management in Bournemouth provides an example.

Promote more sustainable transport: Transport and traffic management is a major issue for sustainable tourism, including:

— Encouraging use of less polluting transport, with global and local benefits; and

— Reducing traffic congestion, noise, and related problems.

Actions should address transport to and within destinations, and should cover information and marketing as well as physical provision. Examples include :

— Promoting walking and cycling routes and related marketing initiatives in most of the case study areas;

— Provision of integrated transport services on the Bournemouth seafront;

— Gradual replacement of rental cars with electric vehicles in Marie-Galante; and

— More active promotion by destinations and enterprises of ways to reach them by public transport, including offering pick-up services.

Conserve and promote natural and cultural heritage resources: Relevant actions here cover both control and management activity and positive use of tourism to support conservation. Examples include:

— Conservation and restoration projects at specific sites;

— Visitor management initiatives;

— Promotion of natural and cultural heritage themes and features to visitors ;

— Methods of raising more support from tourism for conservation, including use of admission charges and encouraging voluntary donations; and

— Improving information and interpretation, including developing events programmes and training local people as guides, as in Marie-Galante.

Help tourism enterprises to be more sustainable: Much of the responsibility for reducing energy and water consumption, waste and pollution, as well as securing more local economic and social benefits, rests with individual tourism enterprises. They can be helped to make their operations more sustainable through a variety of actions, including:

— Training courses and one-to-one advice;

— Provision of guidance manuals supplemented by relevant local information; and

— Financial support for new or existing enterprises adopting sustainability principles.

Use appropriate certification schemes: Recognition of enterprises that fulfil specified sustainability criteria, through awards and labels, can serve as an incentive as well as raising awareness amongst visitors. In some regions of the world, there has been a proliferation of eco-labels related to tourism. A sensible approach at the destination level involves:

— Making use of existing national or wider ecolabeling schemes where they exist, possibly with some local embellishment, as with hotel certification in Storstrøm County and Winchester;

— Further expanding ecolabeling in relation to other types of tourism, and seeking national recognition for this, as was done with holiday houses on Storstrøm; and

— Seeking to integrate ecolabeling with more general quality labelling procedures, as in the new national scheme in England, to which Winchester and Bournemouth relate.

Further consideration should be given to seeking recognition, awards, and accreditation for destinations as a whole for their sustainable approach to tourism. This has been a motivating factor for Bournemouth, and part of Storstrøm County has been a pilot area for the Destination 21 initiative in Denmark.

Prioritise markets that strengthen economic returns: Many sustainable tourism strategies seek to maximise the economic return they get from tourism without generating significant increases in visitation, especially in the high season where the destination may be operating near capacity. This goal may influence the selection of markets to prioritise in promotion and product development strategies. Examples include:

— Encouraging longer-stay tourism rather than day visitors;

— Seeking higher-spending, year-round visitors, as with Bournemouth's strategy to attract conference tourism; and

— Promoting special tourism offers out of season, such as "Calvià, the European Winter".

Promote the use of local products and integration with other sectors: Local Agenda 21 calls for an integrated approach to sustainable development. Moreover, minimising the leakage of visitor spending from a destination is often seen as an important strategic priority in sustainable tourism strategies. Tourism can help to support other sectors by increasing demand for services and adding a source of income to individuals and small businesses.

Promoting local food to visitors and tourism enterprises and developing local gastronomy, including traditional recipes, can benefit the local economy, cultural traditions, and landscapes. Winchester has been influencing tourism suppliers to develop their own health-oriented products, promoting farmers' markets and other local and organic food producers.

Spread tourism benefits and opportunities to all: Social equity is an important principle of LA21. Opportunities for local people to benefit from tourism should be pursued without discrimination. In addition to the participatory measures, relevant action includes:

— Promoting employment opportunities widely throughout the community;

— Providing necessary skills training;

— Seeking to improve pay and conditions;

— Pursing equal employment opportunity policies with respect to race, gender, disability, etc.;

— Making tourism and leisure facilities available to local residents.

Equity principles should also apply to visitors. Relevant action includes:

— Improving accessibility to the destination and its facilities for people with disabilities;

— Promoting a wide selection of accommodation and attractions with a range of prices;

— Maintaining surveys of visitor satisfaction and other feedback processes;

— Taking steps to meet the needs of different types of visitor.

Examples of attention to detail from the case studies include the provision of non-smoking beaches in

Bournemouth and links between the tourism department and the crime prevention group in Winchester.

Strengthen communication with visitors and local residents: Effective communication is essential to achieve sustainability objectives. This should apply to both local residents and visitors. Examples include:

— Bringing out the special environmental and cultural qualities and distinctiveness of the destination through image-building and marketing campaigns;

— Providing detailed information to visitors on both the qualities and the sensitivities of the local natural and cultural heritage, and guidance on how to preserve it;

— Seeking financial and other active support from residents and visitors;

— Engaging local media in putting across the sustainability issues and action being taken.

For example, providing quality information to visitors before and after their arrival, and communicating with local schools about sustainable tourism issues, are part of the LA21 programme in Winchester.

Promoting Development of Sustainable Tousim with LA21 Process

This section presents a summary of action to be taken by governments at an international, national and local level to support a LA21 approach to tourism in desti nations.

International Level

Organisations that work at the international level (UNEP, UNDP, UNESCO, WTO, WTTC, and ICLEI, among others) have an important role to play in helping local authorities and stakeholder groups in destinations in the sustainable development and management of tourism. These organisations should:

— Identify and better disseminate examples of good practice from tourist destinations

— established, recent and emerging - throughout the world that have embarked on LA21 processes (or similar approaches under a different name).

— Support the creation of networks of sustainable tourist destinations, either worldwide or within global regions. The main function of these networks will be to exchange ideas and knowledge.

— Identify policy and planning tools and training requirements that will assist local authorities and destination management organisations to apply LA21 processes to sustainable tourism development and management.

— Prepare and circulate guidelines and advisory material, and promote training and capacity building activities, to meet this goal.

— Encourage more awareness of and response to sustainability issues within the tourism industry, and publicise good examples of partnerships between private companies and local authorities in destinations.

— Identify and support pilot projects to test approaches and guidelines, as well as public/private partnerships and voluntary initiatives based on capacity, willingness and feasibility.

— Gain - and share - more information on the market response to destinations and products that reflect concern for sustainability, such as high-quality environments and cultural distinctiveness.

— Support campaigns to influence international public opinion and tourists' awareness of sustainability issues, including the promotion of codes of conduct and other voluntary initiatives.

— Identify and promote the use of suitable accreditation and certification schemes.

National Authorities

National authorities have an important role to play in creating the conditions for more sustainable development of domestic and incoming tourism, and providing support for local destinations involved in LA21 processes. They should:

— Build national strategies for sustainable tourism based on dialogue with the private sector, local authorities and NGOs.

— Use their statutory powers, particularly on transport matters, to create the conditions for more sustainable tourism.

— Ensure that national tourism organisations and tourism ministries are actively engaged in addressing sustainable development issues in cooperation with environmental ministries and NGOs.

— Encourage all local authorities to prepare Local Agenda 21 strategies and action plans.

— Mount a campaign to encourage local communities to include tourism in their LA 21 strategies, and to reflect LA 21 processes in their tourism strategies. This should include providing information and support.

— Strengthen capacity building for sustainable tourism in local communities.

— Encourage networking among communities most engaged in sustainable tourism development, nationally and within tourist regions.

Local Authorities

All local authorities should be concerned about the sustainable development of their communities. Tourism may play a greater or lesser part, according to the area's location, resources, market circumstances and the general desires and aspirations of the community.

The local authorities should:

— Initiate and support Local Agenda 21 processes, leading to a LA21 strategy and action plan for their area.

— Ensure that tourism is included in the LA 21 process, strategy and action plan. This should be the case with all areas, irrespective of the level of priority that may initially or subsequently be given to tourism.

— If appropriate, and where tourism is a significant issue, prepare separate sustainable tourism strategies and action plans. These should reflect and be associated with the wider LA21 strategy.

— Ensure that all relevant branches of the local authority are involved in planning and managing sustainable tourism in the context of LA21, with leadership and coordination provided at a senior political and executive level.

— Ensure that tourism enterprises, including tour operators and local service providers, who understand the realities of the market place and of running a viable business are involved in planning sustainable development that includes tourism.

— Establish structures to enable tourism, environmental, and community stakeholders to work together on the general Local Agenda 21 for the sustainable development of the area, and on strategies for sustainable tourism associated with it.

— Develop and maintain permanent partnerships for ongoing tourism management in destinations. These should reflect environmental and community interests as well as tourism interests.

— Consult with and involve the wider community and visitors in these processes.

— Develop a widely accepted long-term vision of tourism in the context of the sustainable development of the local area, and identify actions to achieve this vision.

— Give equal attention to economic, environmental, and social impacts of tourism in strategies and actions.

— Integrate sustainable tourism into more broadly applicable planning and management tools and functions, such as spatial planning, environmental management, economic development, and marketing and information services.

— Set clear goals, targets, and indicators for sustainable tourism and regularly monitor and communicate performance and progress with respect to them.

— Work with relevant stakeholders on a set of agreed-upon actions. Give attention to: planning and development control; transport; conservation and promotion of natural and cultural heritage; influencing and assisting private sector enterprises; reducing economic leakage and integrating with other sectors; ensuring an equitable distribution of benefits and opportunities to local residents and visitors; strengthening communication with all concerned; and other issues as may be determined locally.

8

Towards Sustainable Tourism

Tourism can be considered one of the most remarkable socio-economic phenomena of the twentieth century. From an activity "enjoyed by only a small group of relatively well-off people" during the first half of the last century, it gradually became a mass phenomenon during the post-World War II period, particularly from the 1970s onwards.It now reaches larger and larger numbers of people throughout the world, and is a source of employment for a significant segment of the labour force.

Although domestic tourism currently accounts for approximately 80 per cent of all tourist activity, many countries tend to give priority to international tourism because, while the former basically involves a regional redistribution of national income, the latter has now become the world's largest source of foreign exchange receipts.

According to the latest figures compiled by the World Tourism Organization (WTO), foreign exchange earnings from international tourism reached a peak of US$ 476 billion in 2000, which was larger than the export value of petroleum products, motor vehicles, telecommunications equipment or any other single category of product or service. International tourist arrivals grew at an annual average rate of 4.3 per cent during the 1990s, despite major international political and economic crises, such as the Gulf War and the Asian financial crisis.

According to the latest WTO figures, compiled with data received up to August 2001, the turn of the millennium recorded one of the most impressive annual growth rates in international tourism. As Table 1 shows, all regions of the world recorded significant growth in international tourism in 2000, during which the number of international arrivals grew at an extraordinary rate of 7 per cent to reach almost 700 million arrivals.

Table 1: International Tourist Arrivals by Region, 1990-2000

	Region	Million	Arrivals
	1990	1999	2000
Africa	15.0	26.5	27.6
Americas	92.9	122.2	128.5
East Asia & Pacific	54.6	97.6	110.6
Europe	282.7	380.2	403.2
Middle East	9.0	18.2	21.2
South Asia	3.2	5.8	6.4
World	457.3	650.4	697.5

The September 2001 terrorist attacks in the United States, however, appear to have had a more serious impact on the tourist sector than any other major international crisis in recent decades. The attacks had a particularly severe impact on air transport, business travel and long-haul travel. Worldwide travel reservations were estimated to have dropped by 15 per cent at the end of October 2001, although not every destination nor every part of the tourism sector was badly affected.

For example, while air transport and luxury hotels have suffered from considerable fall in demand, travel within the same country or region, as well as travel by rail and road, appear to have weathered the worst effects of the crisis, or even benefited from it: Nevertheless, initial forecasts of 3-4 per cent rise in international tourist arrivals for 2001, made before the September 2001 attacks, were subsequently revised downwards to around a 1 per cent increase over the 2000 figures.

The latest data, released by WTO in January 2002, show that there was a sharp decline of 1.3 per cent in international arrivals, to a total of less than 690 million, in 2001.Given that the northern hemisphere summer holiday season was coming to end by the time the attacks took place, this significant drop confirms that the short-term impacts of the attacks were devastating to international tourism as a whole.

The last four months of 2001, in fact, recorded a drop of almost 11 per cent in arrivals worldwide and substantial decreases in all regions of the world.It is worth noting, however, that this considerable fall in international arrivals was caused not only by a widespread fear of traveling generated by the attacks - particularly in airplanes and to certain destinations - but also by a downturn in the world economy. The economic downturn that began in the United States during the first half of 2001 had already been affecting the tourism sector before the terrorist attacks were carried out. The attacks merely aggravated the economic slowdown already under way.

According to the most recent United Nations economic forecasts,growth of only 1.5 per cent in gross world product (GWP) is expected in 2002, as compared to 1.3 per cent last year. Such a modest improvement is linked to a number of economic uncertainties, notably the high dependency of the global economy on the recovery of the United States. Higher rates of population growth would thus make 2002 the second consecutive year with no real growth in per capita GWP. This, in turn, is also likely to undermine the short-term prospects for a recovery in international tourism, at least until mid-2002, when the summer holiday season begins in the northern hemisphere, and probably until the end of the year. Although much will depend on the evolution of the world economy during this year, it is also likely that some destinations will experience a prolonged decline in tourism revenues regardless of any world economic improvements.

In the medium and long term, however, international tourism is expected to resume its rapid growth, in view of rising living standards and discretionary incomes, falling real costs of travel, expansion and improvement of various transport modes, increasing amounts of free time and other factors.

The World Tourism Organization has recently reiterated its long-term forecasts, made before the September 2001 attacks, of an average annual growth rate in international arrivals of over 4 per cent in the period up to 2020.The number of international arrivals is thus expected to reach the striking mark of 1 billion by 2010 and 1.6 billion by 2020.

Countries and regions where the economy is driven by the tourism industry are becoming increasingly concerned with the environmental, as well as the socio-cultural problems associated with unsustainable tourism. As a result, there is now increasing agreement on the need to promote sustainable tourism development to minimize its environmental impacts and to ensure more sustainable management of natural resources. The concept of sustainable tourism, as developed in the United Nations sustainable development process, refers to tourist activities "leading to management of all resources in such a way that economic, social and aesthetic needs can be fulfilled while maintaining cultural integrity, essential ecological processes, biological diversity and life support systems."These sustainability concerns are, therefore, beginning to be addressed by governments at national, regional and local, as well as international, levels. In addition, given the leading role of the private sector in the tourism industry in most countries, many initiatives have also been taken by this sector.

Policy Areas of Sustainable Tourism

Broadly speaking, the main policy areas regarding sustainable tourism are:

(a) the promotion of national strategies for sustainable tourism development, including the decentralization of environmental management to regional and local levels,

(b) the use of both regulatory mechanisms and economic instruments,

(c) the support for voluntary initiatives by the industry itself, and

(d) the promotion of sustainable tourism at the international level.

National and Regional Strategies

Generally speaking, the main priority for national and regional governments is to incorporate tourism planning and development effectively into overall sustainable development strategies. For example, regional development strategies for areas containing water resources that are potentially attractive to tourism, should carefully consider the availability of those resources in an integrated manner that considers all potential water users. Government policies to promote the domestic tourism industry and to attract foreign direct investment should also ensure that tourism is properly planned and managed so as to minimize adverse environmental impacts and its use of natural resources.

Since the environmental impacts of tourism development are primarily felt at the local and regional levels, national Governments need to promote decentralization of public environment management to the regional and municipal levels. Given that in many countries, local and regional governments already have important responsibilities for tourism development, central Governments should also support capacity building programmes at lower levels in order to enable local and regional authorities to better respond to the challenges of sustainable tourism development in the areas under their jurisdiction. National and local governments also need to develop clear strategies to monitor progress towards sustainable tourism.

Last but far from least, governments at all levels can greatly benefit from working in partnership with all major stakeholders, including local communities, to ensure their active participation in tourism planning, development and management, as well as in the sharing of benefits.Participation of local communities in decision-making and sharing of benefits also helps to generate better awareness of the environmental costs of tourism and thus provides strong incentives to conserve natural resources and protect local environmental assets.

Governments, together with the tourism industry and other stakeholders, should also promote or support various efforts to raise public awareness about the impact of tourists on destinations, to promote respect for local communities and their cultures and to protect the environment. Such public awareness campaigns often succeed in promoting positive behavioural changes not only in tourists, but also in tourism workers and host communities as a whole.

Regulatory Mechanisms and Economic Instruments

Sustainable tourism can also be promoted by a careful mix of government policies comprising both direct regulation and market-based instruments, although financial incentives that encourage environmentally damaging activities, such as energy subsidies, should be reduced or removed. The major challenge for governments is, therefore, to formulate and effectively apply an appropriate mix of regulatory and economic instruments for both sustainable natural resources management and environmental protection.

The most direct tool for promoting sustainable tourism involves the use of regulatory mechanisms, such as, integrated land-use planning and coastal zone management. In many cases, it may be necessary to protect coastlines through rigid building restrictions, such as, existing legislation in several Mediterranean countries that bans any buildings within a defined distance from the coast. It is also essential that environmental regulations be applied transparently throughout the tourism sector, regardless of business size, type of tourism activity concerned or location.

Mass tourism, in particular, should be carefully monitored, regulated and sometimes even prohibited in ecologically fragile areas. In protected areas, such as national parks and natural world heritage sites, tourism activities should be strictly subject to the preservation of biological diversity and ecosystems, not stressing their limited capacity to absorb human presence without becoming damaged or degraded.

In addition to regulation, governments should also consider the use of economic instruments to promote sustainable tourism, including in remote regions where institutional capacity for environmental regulation may be limited. In fact, it can be argued that market-based mechanisms, which apply monetary values to environmental assets, are more efficient for environmental management than government regulation, even at the global level.

Since the tourism industry consumes significant amounts of natural resources, economic pricing of scarce local resources -together with the phasing-out of existing subsidies that encourage wasteful consumption - will help to ensure that the true costs of these resources are adequately incorporated into tourist activities.

Prices that reflect the economic value of water and energy, for example, will promote their efficient use and conservation, and provide additional revenue that can be used to improve the management of those resources.Pollution taxes can also be applied on the amounts of liquid and solid waste generated, as a means to reduce discharges and to generate funds for proper treatment and disposal. Similarly, market-based instruments can also be used effectively for the sustainable use of marine natural resources.Economic instruments, such as user fees and tourist taxes, can actually be used to better internalise environmental costs and thus to promote broader environmental protection objectives.

As it is well known, one of the main reasons why markets fail is that important environmental costs, such as pollution, are not reflected in the prices of goods and services. In a free-market economy, individual economic agents will only attempt to maximize their own utility or profit; external costs will thus not be reflected in prices. If total production costs do not incorporate full environmental costs, resources will be allocated inefficiently, both within countries and globally. One way to deal with externalities is thus to internalize them through taxes so that the full costs of production are reflected in prices.One well-known example of charging user fees to support environmental conservation is the

Bonaire protected marine areas in the Netherlands Antilles.This was one of the first protected marine parks in the Caribbean to become entirely self-financing through the levying of admission fees on scuba divers. The (private) diving industry in Bonaire was initially opposed to the levy because of its potential negative impacts on future demand and revenues, against the background of intense competition offered by many Caribbean diving destinations.

The system, however, has been an unqualified success since it was introduced in January 1992 because many divers (and an increasing number of tourists in general) are willing and able to pay higher prices to support environmental protection. Fees from this scheme also support the active management of the park's coral reef and mangrove ecosystems, as well as educational activities and orientation sessions for divers.

Voluntary Industry Initiatives

Tourism services in most countries are provided primarily by the private sector, which tends to oppose greater government regulation and taxation of the industry on the grounds that they are ultimately detrimental to efficiency, competitiveness and profits. The predominantly private tourism industry has thus developed several self-regulation and voluntary initiatives to promote greater environmental sustainability.

These include waste and pollution reduction schemes, voluntary codes of conduct, industry awards and eco-labels for sustainable tourism. In addition, environmental management schemes to encourage responsible practices have been promoted in various sub-sectors, including hotel and catering, recreation and entertainment, transportation, travel agencies and tour operators.

For example, the World Travel and Tourism Council (WTTC), the main international industry association, has developed an environmental management programme (Green Globe), for both travel and tourism companies and tourism destinations, aimed to raise the level of environmental awareness and to provide a low-cost practical means for improving the environmental performance of the industry. It is also responsible for ECoNETT, an internet-based tool that provides an extensive information resource on all tourism and environmental issues.

Another innovative global programme is the International Hotel Environment Initiative (IHEI), led by a council of leading international hotel chains, aimed to promote environmental management in the hotel industry, which is one of the main consumers of resources and sources of waste. Such initiatives are particularly important not only because they can lead to significant reductions of water and energy consumption, as well as liquid and solid waste, but also because they promote positive behavioural changes in both tourists and employees. In addition, they can lead to improved economic efficiency and increased profitability.

At the regional level, it is worth noting the successful implementation of the Blue Flag Programme, which now extends to 18 countries in Europe, in providing an incentive to protect and improve the quality of beaches and coasts.Under this programme, environmental standards at individual beaches in Europe are assessed by measuring compliance with acceptable concentrations of a range of pollutants to ensure clean bathing water. Beaches are also judged by their compliance with guidelines dealing with litter management, the availability of sanitary and beach safety facilities, and environmental education. Beaches that meet these stringent criteria receive Blue Flag awards, which also serve as a marketing tool to attract tourists.Despite these helpful initiatives of the tourism industry to improve its standards of environmental management and protection, the very proliferation of such voluntary codes of conduct and eco-label awards at global, regional and local levels - which are not, in any case, adopted or recognized by all industry enterprises - can sometimes lead to confusion and difficulty to evaluate and compare them.

While national and regional governments should fully support these voluntary initiatives and encourage the dissemination of the best practices in the private tourism industry, there is also a role for independent supervision, monitoring and comparative assessment by relevant government agencies. In addition, trustworthy codes of conduct, transparent eco-label awards and internationally agreed programmes of action for sustainable tourism are required at the international level. The international community has a particularly crucial role to play in developing a set of internationally recognized accreditation and monitoring systems for assessing the sustainability of tourism services around the world.

International Activities Supporting Sustainable Tourism

Although tourism was not specifically addressed in Agenda 21 - the international programme of action on sustainable development agreed on at the 1992 Earth

Summit in Rio de Janeiro (Brazil)- its growing economic importance, significant use of natural resources and environmental impact all contributed to its gradual introduction into the international sustainable development agenda over the past ten years.

One of the first concrete sectoral programmes of action arising from the increasing cooperation between the tourism industry and inter-governmental agencies was 'Agenda 21 for the Travel and Tourism Industry,' an action plan for sustainable tourism development jointly launched by the World Tourism Organization, the above-mentioned WTTC and the Earth Council in 1996.

Among its innovative key objectives are the estimation of the economic value for resources, such as wildlife, natural areas and cultural heritage, "whose conservation would otherwise be seen as having no financial value," and the establishment of "essential infrastructure, such as water treatment plants, for residents as well as visitors ... (in order to) stimulate other economic activities."Many tourism-based communities and regions have also formulated their own 'Agenda 21s' at the local and regional levels.

In 1997, the United Nations General Assembly, at its special session to review the five-year implementation of Agenda 21, decided that there was a need to consider the importance of tourism in the context of Agenda 21 and to "develop an action-oriented international programme of work on sustainable tourism."This request was followed up during the seventh annual session of the United Nations Commission for Sustainable Development (CSD), held in New York in 1999, which discussed tourism as an economic sector and held a multi-stakeholder dialogue on the topic.

The Commission adopted an international work programme on sustainable tourism development, which is due to be reviewed during the forthcoming World Summit for Sustainable Development in Johannesburg (South Africa) later this year, as part of the ten-year review of progress achieved since the Earth Summit.The CSD also invited the World Tourism Organization to seek further input from the private sector, non-governmental organizations and other stakeholders in the further development of its proposed global code of ethics that had been drafted in consultation with the industry over the previous two years.

The final 'Global Code of Ethics for Tourism, introduced by the World Tourism Organization in late 1999, sets a frame of reference for the responsible and sustainable development of international tourism.It includes nine articles outlining the basic rules for governments, tour operators, developers, travel agents, workers, as well as host communities and the tourists themselves.

The tenth article deals with implementation and includes a proposed mechanism for conciliation, through the creation of a World Committee on Tourism Ethics made up of representatives of each region of the world and representatives of each group of stakeholders in the tourism sector, governments, the private sector, and labour and non-governmental organizations.

The United Nations General Assembly adopted the Global Code of Ethics for Tourism at the end of 2001.Although progress has been achieved over the past ten years, one of the key remaining challenges for the international community is to devise ways and means to assist developing countries to ensure that their tourism industries become more internationally competitive without damaging their natural resources and environmental assets base.

This will require, amongst other things, greater technical and financial assistance, including human resources development, institutional capacity building and the transfer of environmentally sound technologies to many developing countries. The international community could also support the wider use of 'debt-fornature swaps', through which a portion of the foreign debt of developing countries is purchased at a discount by various international partners in exchange for the debtor's country investment of an agreed sum of local currency in environmental protection projects.

As stressed above, tourism is expected to resume its rapid growth in the future because of improved living standards, rising incomes and amounts of free time, the falling real cost of travel, and improved transportation around the world. This growth can be harnessed not only for the enjoyment of tourists themselves but, more importantly, for maximizing economic benefits and thus increasing the living standards of host communities and countries.

At the same time, it is bound to have negative environmental and socio-cultural impact on those communities, whose involvement in tourism planning, development and management can be crucial to minimizing the impact. The major challenge for the international community is, therefore, not only to minimize the negative impact of tourism but also to ensure that the economic benefits of tourism can contribute to environmental protection and the sustainable use of natural resources.

The International Year of Ecotourism - officially launched at the United Nations headquarters in New York on 28 January 2002- offers an ideal opportunity not only to review ecotourism experiences around the world, but also to promote worldwide recognition of the important role of sustainable tourism in the broader international sustainable development agenda. Ecotourism is one of the fastest growing segments of the tourism sector and further rapid growth is expected in the future. There is, however, little agreement about its exact meaning because of the wide variety of so-called ecotourism activities provided by many different tour operators and enjoyed by an equally broad range of diverse tourists. Its main features include

(a) all forms of nature tourism aimed at the appreciation of both the natural world and the traditional cultures existent in natural areas,

(b) deliberate efforts to minimize the harmful human impacts on the natural and socio-cultural environment and

(c) support for the protection of natural and cultural assets and the well-being of host communities.

In other words, if carried out responsibly, ecotourism can be a valuable means for promoting the socio-economic development of host communities while generating resources for the preservation of natural and cultural assets. In this way, ecologically fragile areas can be protected with the financial returns of ecotourism activities made by both the public and private sectors. In many developing countries, ecotourism has been particularly successful in attracting private investments for the establishment of privately owned natural parks and nature reserves.

Many of such reserves are well-managed, self-financed and environmentally responsible, even when profit remains the main motivation behind the operation of a private reserve.In this way, the tourism industry can help to protect and even rehabilitate natural assets, and thus contribute to the preservation of biological diversity and ecological balance.

However, if not properly planned, managed and monitored, the concept of ecotourism can be distorted for purely commercial purposes and even for promoting ecologically-damaging activities by large numbers of tourists in natural areas. Given their inadequate physical infrastructure and limited capacity to absorb mass tourism, the fragile land and ocean ecosystems of many developing countries can be literally overwhelmed by large numbers of tourists. It is increasingly recognized, therefore, that unsustainable ecotourism activities may threaten the very natural environment upon which they depend. There is, in fact, a crucial distinction between ecotourism and sustainable tourism: while the former can be broadly defined as an alternative, nature-based type of tourism, the above-mentioned sustainability principles must be applied to all types of tourism activities and all segments of the tourism industry.

At a campsite on the long trekking route to Concordia and K-2 base camp in northern Pakistan, there is a presumably 'politically correct' sign that says: "Take nothing but photos; Leave nothing but footprints." If tourists follow those instructions, but do so insensitively or in mass numbers, those seemingly inoffensive acts can disturb local cultural values and ecological balance, respectively. It should be clear by now that even ecotourism activities can cause adverse ecological impacts, particularly if they are not properly managed or if they involve tourist numbers beyond the local carrying capacity. After all, there is no paradise on Earth.

Steps to Sustainable Tourism

Sustainable tourism is a long-term goal. At its heart is what makes a region, place or tourism product special. This section offers a step-by-step approach to foster partnerships and to achieve benefits for tourism and conservation interests. It can be used by tourism operators, local government, tourism organisations, heritage managers, regional development bodies, park managers, communities, consultants and all those interested in fostering a sustainable approach to tourism.

STEP 1. What do to do?

Whether you're using this process in relation to a region, a particular place or a tourism product, your first step is to determine what you would like to achieve and to understand the context of your project.

The statement of aim that you produce will become an important reference for briefings, consultation, media communications and proposals, as it will help others to clearly understand what you're trying to achieve. If a number of people are involved, you must all agree on your aims before going any further.

Aims

A clearly defined aim will guide the work ahead. It can be as simple as you like and can be worded many different ways such as in a vision statement, mission statement or statement of purpose. Invest a little time in making sure this statement is tight, clear and achievable.

In developing your aim, consider:

— what are we aiming to achieve

— in the short term?

— in the long term?

— why do we need to do this?

— what time frames are we working to?

What is the context for your region, place or project?

To help you and others better understand the context of

the region, place or project, you will need to set the scene in a brief overview statement. This statement should cover:

— social setting

— economic conditions

— current political climate

— natural environment setting and

— cultural considerations.

Some of the key questions you may need to answer succinctly are:

— what are the key natural and cultural assets for tourism?

— what are the current visitor numbers?

— what is the potential for future growth in visitor numbers?

— how well is the current situation working?

— is the place or region appropriate for tourism use and development?

If at all possible clearly identify common ground or potential areas/points of conflict between those interested in the place/project. Defining common ground early in the process can be important in assisting progress. How to manage issues and conflicts will be explored in later steps.

Step 2. Who is, could be or needs to be involved?

It is important to find out who is concerned about and responsible for tourism, environment and heritage issues relating to your place or region. If you systematically and strategically identify and involve those with a stake in your place, region or tourism product, you will:

— ensure the right people are involved in planning and future activities

— help determine heritage significance of places involved

— help make sure all the important issues are considered

— help to decide what future actions are realistic and will best meet everyone's needs and

— help build support for regional plans, management plans and development proposals.

This step is important as it will underpin all future steps and will need to be revisited and updated continually.

Initially, everyone who is, could be or needs to be involved or considered in future decisions should be identified and the nature of their interest noted. From here, various forms of consultation, as appropriate, can be considered and this can then lead some form of involvement in the process, project or business.

Who are the stakeholders?

Determine who is, should or could be involved by listing all potential stakeholders.

You can identify stakeholders by:

— talking to people

— reading existing reports and

— if necessary, publicly or formally seeking interested persons or organisations.

Start using existing networks and communication forums to identify the people who might be involved. Ask your colleagues:

— who else should I talk to?

— who is not involved who should be?

Some or all of the following questions may help you to identify the people, groups and organisations who may need to be informed, consulted or involved in some way. Understanding the nature of the interest of each stakeholder helps, whether it is statutory, professional, economic, cultural or personal. Depending on their interest, stakeholders may just need to be kept in mind in future steps, others will need to be included in some form of consultation and a smaller set will need to be involved. The essential or key stakeholders should be identified as early as possible.

How to consult and involve people

Informing and involving people can be challenging and time consuming but can make a huge difference to successful projects, plans and tourism products. Consultation processes can be targeted at your key stakeholders for specific purposes, or might be designed to generally inform the community, build support and seek willing involvement. There are many different consultation techniques. Choosing the best one for you will depend on the context, type of people involved and the available human and financial resources. Some techniques are formal, others are targeted and specific. The range of techniques includes, but is not limited to:

— community meetings

— interviews

— public exhibitions, displays and information sheets

— advisory committees

— media placements seeking input

— written submissions

— telephone polls and surveys
— focus groups
— open days
— guided information tours
— conferences or workshops
— residents' feedback sessions
— visual mapping
— pictorial and photographic illustration.

If you would like help in developing your consultation approaches, you may like to engage someone who is trained or experienced in consultation techniques. Working out the appropriate people to involve is often a matter of common sense, but it can be important to involve people other than the usual suspects. Sometimes these people can be a breath of fresh air, and bring with them new and interesting perspectives.

How to develop effective working relationships

Several other factors may make a big difference in establishing or developing effective working relationships, such as:

— identifying the 'drivers' or champions
— identifying the key people to be involved in regular communication and
— identifying important partnerships.

Drivers and champions

Every project or process needs someone to coordinate activities, bring people together and be the central contact point. This individual may be the initial person to get the process rolling before handing it on to others, or they could be nominated as the coordinator by superiors or a project team. This person, along with other contact people, should be clearly identified, and all key stakeholders notified of their role, and provided with their contact details.

Project teams, working groups or steering committees

Where possible, use and build on existing communication mechanisms to coordinate work. If a suitable consultative group does not already exist, it may be useful to set up a working group to address issues relevant to your region, place or tourism product. The aim of the working group should be to communicate across organisations, integrate the needs of tourism, heritage and the environment and foster support for the process.

Possible participants for a working group

Appoint members and use them as conduits for information into the group and out to the broader community. Your group can be as formal or informal as you like. It can provide a focal point for reporting and communication between people, accessing information, exploring options, making decisions and communicating to the broader community. It should reflect all key interests, and should involve key people or organisations at the core of decision-making.

Developing partnerships

Successful tourism often requires resources that no one organisation can offer so partnerships can be an effective tool when dealing across tourism and heritage issues. They can help to build support, and to coordinate rather than duplicate efforts. Taking a partnership approach early on, may help you when seeking approvals and may ensure that you have all the right information as a project progresses.

The key steps to developing partnerships are:

1. identifying what key partnerships will help you to achieve your goals
2. identifying the people who are or should be involved
3. building the relationships
4. developing mutual understandings of issues and the natural and cultural heritage involved
5. jointly developing goals and objectives
6. expressing commitment to the partnership, and to implementing agreed future actions.

The following pointers may help you to establish your group:

— decide on the role of the working group, how often will it meet and what is expected of its members

— try to keep your group small rather than large as it is likely to be more effective, but remember also to let others know what you are doing encourage working group members to promote the process by spreading news about progress and key issues

— nominate a contact person and/or coordinator, or a system to rotate the role and

— make sure everyone has their say, set meetings with a clear agenda, time limits and defined outcomes.

Appoint members and use them as conduits for information into the group and out to the broader community. Your group can be as formal or informal as you like. It can provide a focal point for reporting and communication between people, accessing information, exploring options, making decisions and communicating to the broader community. It should reflect all key interests, and should involve key people or organisations at the core of decision-making.

Step 3. What is known?

Information is a powerful tool so drawing together relevant facts and figures will provide a solid grounding for future decisions. As you look for material on planning and managing tourism at heritage places, and the current and potential tourism market, you may find that much useful information already exists.

Where to look

You might have a look at books, newspaper articles, sound recordings, council records, tourism brochures, annual reports, tour operator records, park management plans and research reports. Information can also be found:

— by talking to knowledgeable individuals and through observations, interviews, questionnaires and focus groups

— in local and state libraries

— in private collections

— on websites

— through various local or regional organisations

— in universities

— at heritage site management authorities

— at government departments

— with tour operators.

Step 4. What makes this region, place or product special?

In this step you need to identify the important values of your place, region or product, and the ways in which they are understood and communicated. Places can be special for all kinds of reasons - they may be important to the local community or to the world as a whole.

Tourism, heritage and local community interests will benefit from developing a common understanding of what is significant so that they have a unified approach to presenting local and regional heritage to visitors.

Identifying natural and cultural heritage values

Natural and cultural heritage places are often the key assets for tourism. The unique qualities of a place, or its values, can be a large part of a tourism business and its key selling points.

Understanding the values of your heritage places is essential for effective product development, planning, marketing, management and interpretation. It is also important when considering the appropriateness of introducing or expanding tourism activities at your heritage place. This understanding helps to ensure that future development is as compatible as possible with the ongoing care of the values. You may find that the values have already have been documented by natural and cultural heritage specialists or are known to locals. Heritage professionals have developed considerable expertise and have structured methods (including criteria) for assessing the significance of a place. Information they can offer on aesthetic, historical, scientific, social and spiritual significance will be valuable. Hunt out this information. A good place to start is to check local, state or national heritage registers.

Identifying other values

Other values, aside from those formally recognised by heritage specialists, are also important. These may be the less tangible aspects that make a place, region or experience special to the local community or to visitors. They may relate to its cultural, community, recreational and economic uses.

Additional information on identifying values can be found in the companion volume to this framework, the Protecting Heritage Places Kit, listed at the end of this booklet.

The tourism perspective

Stories based on heritage values, particularly those provided by local people, are often what make a place attractive to visitors. These stories are also what visitors take away with them and share with others when they return home. The combination of values, stories and landscapes, can create a total 'experience' for the visitor. Determining what makes the region, place or product special should take into account all the values that are known. The following questions may help you to identify the special attributes of your region, place or product.

The results of this step can be presented in a statement of why this region, place or product is special. This statement is a blend of identified heritage values and other values which potentially make the region, place or product engaging for visitors. It is called a 'Heritage and Tourism Value Statement'. This statement can be used to develop a common understanding of what is special about a place and the best way to present these values to visitors Once agreed, it can form the basis for stakeholders to move forward to the next step. This statement should be followed by a short outline describing:

1. how well the special values are currently being recognised and communicated to visitors and
2. what added potential exists to use the special values in tourism and interpretation programs.

Step 5. What are the issues?

This step is about identifying all the important issues or factors that might affect what happens in the future. This means talking to people and looking at the information you have collected to date. Tease out the important matters that are unresolved or that will impact on your place, region or tourism product. Before you start, remember:

— issues are not always problems - they can be worked on and with

— identify conflicts in perspectives or issues - flag these for further clarification and analysis so that you can find ways to address them later

— focus on the issues and not the people raising them

— if people have identified issues, make sure these are considered through the next steps. People's views need to be reflected in the process and individuals should also be able to see their input

— in identifying issues, you may come across some which require expert advice or further investigation. This could include professional assessments of the condition of places, market potential, and visitor management and interpretation. Obtaining professional advice or digging out extra information may help to build a sturdier foundation for planning future work, forecasting budgets and preparing for any necessary approvals

— a thorough knowledge of issues will also help you to develop performance measures and monitoring indicators as you address the issues over time.

Ways to identify issues

Identify issues clearly and thoroughly. Where necessary, consider using professional skills and approaches, such as those offered by facilitators experienced or trained in techniques for working with stakeholders and identifying issues. If you are undertaking this step yourself, think of running separate meetings or separate parts of meetings, so that people have a chance to think and talk about issues concerning them. Record what people say. Ensure everyone has an opportunity to express their view.

Further checks that can help you to identify important issues are:

— Revisit step 2 (who is involved?) and consider the issues that might come from different perspectives and stakeholders. If you don't have an understanding of issues from their point of view, how might you find this out?

— Revisit step 3 (what do we know?) to consider issues raised previously. Are there any recommendations that have been made before?

— Revisit step 4 (what is special?) and consider issues that arise when we understand what makes a place, region or tourism product special.

Identifying issues

To help consider and cover the range of issues relevant to both tourism and heritage, it may be useful to consider:

— consumer/visitor experience

— community experience
— environment/heritage management and impacts
— infrastructure issues
— market/marketing issues
— tourism product availability
— economic cost/benefit issues
— training/capacity building
— strategic and resource context
— approvals and regulation.

In considering each of these, it may be useful to look at the following questions to help you consider possible issues. Not all will be relevant to your situation. A thoughtful presentation and discussion of the issues raised by answering the above questions can be drafted under suitable headings such as those above, or whatever form is most appropriate to your region, place or tourism product. Where possible identify the highest priority issues as identified by knowledgeable people or by consensus. This will help you to target the analysis in the next step. Sometimes an issue is broadly identified, but not enough information exists on which to base a reasonable judgement. In this case, either you need to gather more information about the issue, or use some sort of analytical technique to develop a clearer picture. Various types of analysis appropriate for tourism, heritage and business planning are detailed in the next step.

Handling conflicts

It is important to identify areas of conflict, as these can reappear later as barriers to progress or action. Looking beyond the conflict of different ideas and people and getting to the root cause can often help to resolve the issue. Conflict is often inevitable. It can make ideas or projects unworkable, but it may also present opportunities for innovative solutions.

Various methods of conflict resolution and mediation processes exist. Rather than focusing on the particular individuals and their views and creating an adversarial situation, there are ways of working with interests to acknowledge views, explore issues and develop solutions cooperatively.

In some cases informal cooperative and collaborative approaches will be successful, others may require more formal approaches such as negotiation, arbitration or mediation. Using the services of a professional and 'neutral' facilitator can produce a good result.

Keys to managing and resolving conflicts include:

— having an inclusive participatory process

— maintaining open and effective communication

— being responsive and adaptable and

— building consensus between a majority of stakeholders.

Step 6. Analysing issues

Now that the issues have emerged from the last step, you may need to delve further to clarify what is going on. Important issues need to be fully understood if the right decision is to be made about a particular course of action.

Concentrate your efforts on analysing priority issues. If resources are limited you may need to make a judgement based on available information and analysis. Analysis may simply be a matter of presenting a reasoned judgement about an issue with justification of how you came to that position and citing what data or information supports this. More sophisticated analysis may help you to make better business and management decisions, but this can also be time-consuming and costly, so compromises may have to be made. In any case you should clearly state how you have reached your current understanding of the situation.

Many of the methods of analysis described below are standard approaches used in strategic planning. Some of them, such as market analysis, are essential components for business plans. You will need to decide what types of analysis are relevant or appropriate to your situation. The aim of using any analytical technique is to better understand factors at play in what might be a very complex situation. Analysis will also help to further identify and prioritise fundamental issues.

Key analytical methods may include, but are not limited to the following:

— market analysis

— heritage conservation analysis

— SWOT analysis

— situational analysis

— cost-benefit analysis

— priority analysis.

Market analysis

A number of market-related issues would have emerged in the previous step. A market analysis is an analytical summary of how your region, place or product fits into the marketplace. It takes into account the saleability or profitability of a product or service, based on information about the product and the potential market. Market analysis may include an assessment of how your region, place or tourism product compares with existing competition. Are there others around competing for a similar market? What are their strengths? What are yours? Is the market big enough for people to share? How can your region, place or product be presented in the marketplace to maximise the fit between what you can offer and what people want? Basically a market analysis should assess the supply and demand for tourism product, accommodation, transport and associated services relating to your situation. This type of analysis helps in positioning your product intelligently in the marketplace. You can estimate the market potential for a product using information on sales volumes for similar products or in similar regions. Industry statistics collected regularly across Australia may also be available from you state or territory tourism organisation.

Market analysis often includes a forecast of where the market is going. Trends over time may indicate how your product or service may fare in the future. In the summary of your market analysis you should explain the potential for future development opportunities based on market and trend information.

Heritage conservation analysis

In Step 4 you identified the factors that make your place special - its heritage values. In some cases, when the implications of tourism on a heritage place become clearer, you may need to revisit this question with further specific studies on the heritage values, or on particular technical issues that may affect how the site is used. One important type of conservation analysis is a condition analysis. This method uses trained heritage conservation experts to look closely at buildings, Indigenous sites or natural features and assess their physical condition, and their capacity to withstand visitors or other possible indirect impacts.

Situational analysis

This is a description of the context in which tourism is currently occurring. It includes the main determining factors such as the seasonal or geographic flow patterns and the functional relationships at play. Understanding the situation is the first step in designing the response.

A situational analysis involves analysing needs and assets, understanding what works well and what doesn't and the capacity of those involved. Including others in situational analysis helps to build a better understanding of the context or situation.

SWOT analysis (Strengths, Weaknesses, Opportunities and Threats)

This is a very standard way to help identify and consider the issues identified in Step 5. A SWOT analysis is a simple and useful part of many types of strategic plans, including business plans.

In this process you will need to consider the present strengths and weaknesses of your situation and future possibilities for opportunities and threats. Remember, that the weaknesses and threats can become strengths and opportunities if addressed. This analysis will help you to get an overview of key issues, and will help to articulate issues that may not have come out in other ways. It is useful to undertake SWOT analysis after you have collected and considered information from issues identified in the last step.

Cost-benefit analysis

This is a relatively simple and widely used technique. As its name suggests, simply add up the value of the benefits of a particular approach or idea and then subtract its associated costs. Costs are either one-off or ongoing. Benefits generally accumulate over time. Costs and benefits can be financial, environmental and social. Putting a financial value on intangible costs and benefits can be more challenging and highly subjective. Cost-benefit analysis is linked to the concept of the 'triple bottom line' which is used as a framework for measuring and reporting performance against three key areas - economic, social and environmental.

Priority analysis

You can determine priorities in many different ways, but one simple way is to look at the importance and urgency of the issues.

Step 7. Principles or objectives to guide action

Now that you have an understanding of tourism and heritage values and the key issues at play, you need to consider more specifically what you want to achieve. This should be a balance between looking after heritage and developing tourism if, and where, appropriate.

In Steps 2 to 6 you drew together all the relevant background material and knowledge. Using this as your foundation you now need to consider where you want to go in the future. In this step you will develop specific objectives, or if appropriate, a general set of principles, to guide future work.

These principles or objectives, need to deal with the realities of tourism while maintaining and protecting what is special about the area's natural and cultural heritage. It is very important that principles or objectives are agreed by key stakeholders and that they have a high level of ownership. Implementation of the principles works best when people feel they have played an important part in their development.

Principles

In some cases a general set of principles is the most appropriate way to guide the direction and breadth of future work. Principles can be expressed in the form of guidelines, protocols or policy statements. For example, a tourism business might develop a set of responsible tourism principles, or a set of protocols might be developed with Indigenous communities covering issues relating to Indigenous heritage and tourism.

In historic heritage conservation plans, you can often find a statement of 'conservation policies'. Where these policies exist, they should be included in the principles as they are likely to guide the development of heritage tourism.

Objectives

Setting objectives is one of the most common ways of planning for the future. Objectives are sets of short statements that are like goal posts. They are something to aim towards, and can give a clearer focus to your plan and efforts.

Objectives should be written in clear language, be specific, measurable, realistic, and have a time frame. They are an important part of many planning documents, including business plans.

Objectives are created by thinking how you want the future to look. Build into your objectives words which reflect economic and community aspirations as well as the intention to take care of heritage. Objectives should be developed and owned collectively by stakeholders or business partners.

They can be written in several different ways. One approach is to state your intent, for example, "to improve directional signage at...". The other way is to state the desired end result, for example "signs installed at all...". The form you use will depend on personal preference and the context in which they are to be used. You can measure whether or not you have met your objectives by developing indicators or tangible evidence of attaining your goals. You may also want to think about what milestones would help to break down your work into achievable stages. As your work proceeds, any reporting should focus on your progress towards achieving your objectives. This is the means by which you and others can monitor performance.

Step 8. What are your ideas and options?

You will have generated ideas and concepts as you have progressed through Step 3 (what information is there?), Step 4 (what makes this region, place or product special?), Step 5 (identifying issues) and Step 6 (analysing issues). The aims and objectives identified in Step 7 can help you to develop ideas and options in this step. It's likely that you will have many different options and pathways to your final goal or goals. If you are working in a region or community, you may need to consider many possibilities before making a final decision. In planning for tourism the feasibility of one or more options may need to be tested and presented before funding or approvals are granted.

Developing ideas

As you have worked through this process, many ideas will have emerged or will have been put forward by the people with whom you have been working. Now you can bring those ideas forward and show how they might work. You may need to bundle together specific ideas into packages or groups of actions. You will need to take into account key issues and to ensure that you maximise opportunities and manage any threats. If clear ideas and options do not emerge at first, you may need to develop them through discussions, brainstorming sessions, focus groups or workshops.

In general, ideas and options should include:

— the visitor experience
— community engagement
— care of heritage assets
— infrastructure
— marketing
— product development
— stakeholder communication
— training and capacity building and
— necessary resources and support.

Revisit the issues and analysis to remind you of what aspects you need to consider.

Presenting ideas or options for testing

Once you have put together your ideas into a package or proposal that you think will work you can then present this to a group of informed people, a business or project team or a stakeholder group. Use their knowledge and experience to test how your ideas might meet the needs of key interests while also addressing the issues and opportunities of the situation. When presenting the options you should give a realistic assessment of their feasibility and include information on proposed timing and required resources.

Analysing issues further, if needed

When developing your ideas or options, you may

discover that you don't have a clear picture of some important elements. If so, go back to Steps 5 and 6 to gather more information or further analyse your situation. If you have several possible scenarios, you can test how each scenario might fare in light of your market analysis. You might even want to conduct specific market testing of your ideas or product.

Developing recommended option/s

Once you have tested your ideas and gathered any extra information that you need, you can then develop your preferred options. These should be backed up by a clearly reasoned statement supported by the information you have collected in the steps so far. These options can then be presented in a proposal, feasibility study or strategic plan. Good communication and people skills can make a big difference when it comes to convincing others of the benefits of your recommended option/s.

Seeking agreement on preferred option/s

Negotiating over the best course of action can be complicated by tensions between competing interests. Different stakeholders are likely to have different but equally legitimate priorities. At this point it is important to focus on the positive mutual interests that can link tourism, heritage conservation and communities and that can form the basis for cooperation. Once a particular idea or option looks like meeting most people's needs, your next step will be to seek agreement through the necessary formal and informal processes. As you obtain agreements and support, make sure you document this for future reference.

Step 9. How to do it?

The preferred options or ideas from the previous step

now need to be turned into actions that you can implement!

Making new projects or ideas happen may involve many stakeholders, organisations and groups. Even if implementation is the responsibility of one organisation or business, you will probably need to gain the support or approval of others. Whatever your situation, a clear implementation plan is essential. This not only makes sound business sense but is standard practice in project management. This plan can also be called an action plan or a work plan.

In addition to developing this plan, each participating organisation may need to look at its own planning documents to ensure that the implementation plan links to existing planning documents. It may be worth having an overall implementation/action plan for heritage tourism issues as a common agreed framework. The following sample format covers the important implementation issues.

Additional factors

Additional factors that are crucial to address include:

— strategies for political support
— communication
— capacity building
— making links
— staging
— influence.

Strategies for political support - consider and include actions that help build political support for what you want to achieve. Lobbying can be a legitimate and necessary activity.

Communication - good mechanisms for communicating are vital in bringing together diverse interests and helping them to work together. Consider and include any actions or activities that will make this happen. Too often these communication activities are not given the resourcing or attention that they deserve.

Capacity building - while training and staff or community development may be included as an objective of the plan, you may also want to think carefully about whether implementing the plan will need specific training or capacity building. What support or additional capacity do individuals or groups need to participate and play an effective role in implementation?

Making links - consider how different activities can link together to create a whole which is greater than the sum of its parts. Often the most efficient use of resources comes from piggy-backing on other initiatives and pursuing activities with multiple outcomes.

Staging - consider how actions can build up in stages over time to reach the desired result. At times you may need to reach one stepping stone before reassessing where to go next.

Influence - gain the support of other key players and influence other plans or activities to increase your ability to make a difference. Ways of gaining support need to be considered and included in your planning and activities.

Keeping on track

Any strategic plan, development plan or action plan needs to be followed and referred to regularly to be kept relevant. The best way to use a plan is to constantly check and report on progress. You can do this through:

— performance measures or indicators

— monitoring and reporting and

— evaluating and reviewing.

Performance measures or indicators - these can be used to monitor progress and identify what is being achieved They help to demonstrate how well an organisation, program or strategy is meeting its objectives or when actions are not proceeding as planned. They can also show where performance can be improved. Performance indicators can use qualitative and quantitative information. They should be relevant to the program's desired outcomes and objectives, be quantifiable, verifiable and free from bias.

Indicators can be relatively simple, cheap and easy to measure. You can develop these yourself or use existing indicators.

Monitoring and reporting - build into your implementation plan key points at which to check your progress. It is a good idea to give formal progress reports to the group with responsibilities across both tourism and heritage interests. This will help keep attention on what has been achieved and what still needs to be done. Timeframes for monitoring and reporting are important and should be carefully thought through. You need to allow enough time to determine if the outcomes are successful or whether you have made a significant impact. If unforeseen obstacles arise you may want to report sooner rather than later to avert negative consequences. You also need to consider how much time it takes to collect and collate monitoring data. Evaluating and reviewing - your plan should also include a timeframe (three to five years is typical). A major evaluation and review should be conducted at the end of this time. This may lead to the plan being refreshed or the process being repeated to produce a new plan.

Keeping track of progress means that efforts can be redirected and management continually adapted to suit changing circumstances.

Step 10. Statement of directions

This step will help you to:

If you are writing up a plan, this step is simply like the conclusion or executive summary.

It summarises in as succinct a form as possible:

— the key heritage and tourism assets of the region, place or product

— the key issues and

— the agreements and outcomes reached between parties.

If you are using this process to run a meeting or series of meetings, or a major project, this step comes at the end so that all the people involved can see what they have achieved and can be clear about the outcomes. There may also be other creative ways to present your outcomes through images or other forms of communication. Whatever case, you will find this summary very useful for briefing colleagues, superiors and for including in newsletters, electronic information or media materials.

Bibliography

Manning, R. & Powers, L. "Peak and Off-Peak Use: Redistributing the Outdoor Recreation/Tourism Load" in Journal of Travel Research (23:2): 25, 1984.

Marin, R., & Lemieux, G. H., *"Preservation of the environment in the perspective of sustainable development: the case of Costa Rica" in Society and Leisure*. 13 (2): 409-430, 1990.

Mathieson, A. & Wall, G., *Tourism: Economic. Physical. and Social Impacts*. New York: Longman Scientific & Technical, 1982.

McLaren, D., "Community Ecotourism" in Transitions Abroad, March (18:5), 1995.

McNeely, J.A. & Miller, K.R. eds., "National Parks, Conservation and Development: The Role of Protected Areas in Sustaining Society" in World Congress on National Parks, Bali, Indonesia, 1982. Washington, D.C.: Smithsonian Institution Press, 1984.

Metcalfe, D., "Seven Spirit Bay: An Ecotourism Development in Western Amhem Land, Northern Territory" in Ecotourism: Incorporating the Global Classroom. *Paper presented at the International Conference on Ecotourism at University of Queensland*, Brisbane, Australia, 1992.

Miller, M.L. & Ditton, R.B., "Travel, Tourism and Marine Affairs" in Coastal Zone Management Journal (12:1/2): 1-19, 1986.

Norris, R., "Ecotourism in the National Parks of Latin America" in National Parks, January (68: 1 / 2), 1994.

Olindo, P., "The Old Man of Nature Tourism": *Kenya. In Nature Tourism: Managing for the Environment*. Island Press, 23-38, 1991.

Orams, M.B., "Towards a more desirable form of ecotourism" in Tourism Management, February (6:1), 1995.

Patterson, B., *Ecotourism in Environment*, (April): 47-48, 1991.

Pearce, D.G., *Tourism and Environmental Research: A Review" in the International Journal of Environmental Studies* (25): 247-255, 1985.

Ranney, S. A. G., *Wild Places, Wildlife, and Ecotourism: Outdoor Leadership Demands in the New World. National Conference for Outdoor Leaders, Public, Commercial, and Non-profit Partnerships*, 1991.

Reid, L. J. (ed.), "Tourism, Environment, Sustainable Development". *Conference proceedings of the Travel and Tourism Research Association: Canada Chapter*, 1991.

Index